MAKING POTTERY WITHOUT A WHEEL

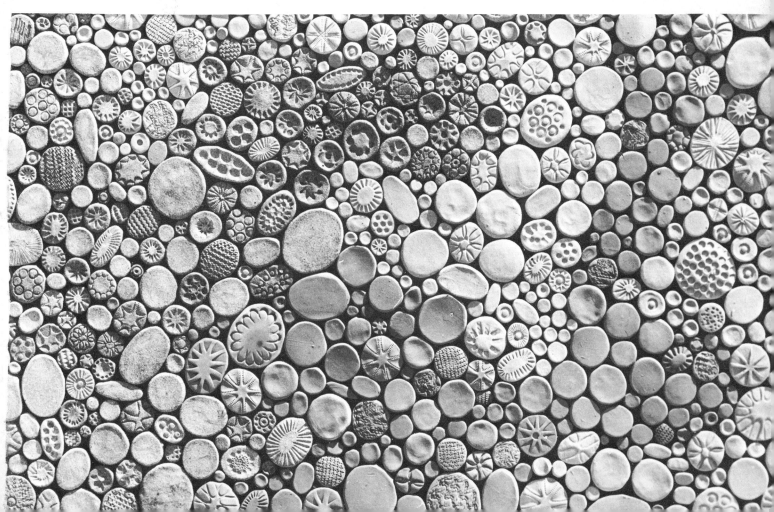

MAKING POTTERY

POTTERY

WITHOUT A WHEEL

Texture and Form in Clay

F. Carlton Ball

and

Janice Lovoos

VNR VAN NOSTRAND REINHOLD COMPANY

NEW YORK CINCINNATI TORONTO LONDON MELBOURNE

*This book is lovingly dedicated to
the Ball family, and to Thor Lovoos.*

Van Nostrand Reinhold Company Regional Offices:
New York   Cincinnati   Chicago   Millbrae   Dallas

Van Nostrand Reinhold Company Foreign Offices:
London   Toronto   Melbourne

Copyright © 1965 by Reinhold Publishing Corporation
Library of Congress Catalog Card Number 65-12977

Photographs by F. Carlton Ball
Designed by Emilio Squeglio
Type set by Lettick Typographic Inc.
Printed by Book Printers, Inc.
Bound by Sendor Bindery, Inc.
Published by Van Nostrand Reinhold Company
450 West 33rd Street, New York, N. Y. 10001
Published simultaneously in Canada by
Van Nostrand Reinhold Ltd.

16   15   14   13   12   11   10   9   8   7   6   5   4

CONTENTS

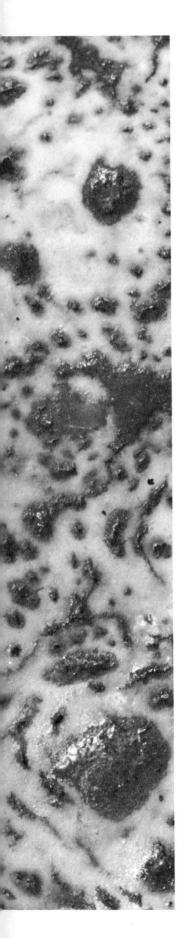

ACKNOWLEDGMENTS

I wish to express my sincere thanks to the pottery students who have helped me with the photography concerned with this book, with special thanks to Floyd Cawthon; to graduate students who have also assisted with the photography and firing of the kilns; to *Ceramics Monthly* magazine for the use of the photographs on coil building.

F. Carlton Ball

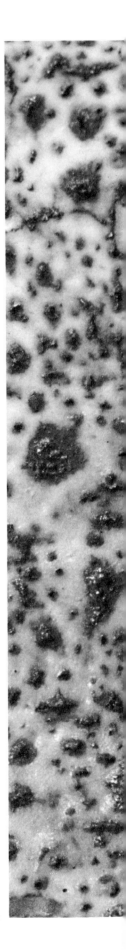

FOREWORD

*"Of clay I am it is most true,
Disdain me not for so are you."*

The big platter on which these words were printed with underglaze many years ago now reposes under glass in a museum in England. To many, the smug statement on the ancient serving dish may be only a harsh leveler of mankind. To potters, however, it is a facetious reminder that the closer we live with materials that come from the earth, the better potters we will be.

In an age with so many technical marvels in art and industry, new trends in ceramics may easily become mere fashions of the moment. At such times it is reassuring that a man of Professor Carlton Ball's ability writes in favor of the less glamorous struggles one faces when learning to work with clays, glazes and surface enrichment.

In this book, Mr. Ball introduces the reader to the methods and idea resources that have inspired his own great achievement in ceramics. Step-by-step he shows the amazing range of forms that may be fashioned from clay using such basic hand-forming methods as coil, slab and mold. Photographs selected from the author's own massive collection help the potter draw from clay the miracles of form, pattern and texture inherent in this elemental medium.

"The *idea* is the thing in making ceramic form. Underglazes, glazes and colored slips are but the raiment of the idea," declares Carlton Ball. "The wheel does what it is forced to do and often requires years of practice." Throwing on a wheel does not appeal to everyone. The wheel produces symmetrical forms only; while the hands, although they can never produce a perfectly symmetrical bowl or a big jar, are able to fashion beautiful and useful forms and to create decorative details impossible on a whirling wheel.

The sources of Carlton Ball's ideas are many. With camera and light he has captured the tenuous beauty of sea anemones in the clear water of tiny lagoons left by receding tides. He has made oblique exposures of wave patterns on sandy shores. Directing attention to the difference between the sea and the desert, he photographs the skeletons of yucca plants that have been eroded by wind and sand. Carlton Ball has also derived patterns from the bizarre rock formations in the agatized wood fragments from petrified forests in Arizona. Photographs of these strange patterns and forms are used later as design motifs.

The change that takes place in the original idea when it is worked out in clay is often dismaying to the amateur who is not yet familiar with the rugged power of clay. The safest, most rewarding way to work, Carlton Ball believes, is to let the clay speak in its own untamed way. His tools are mainly objects he finds. To his students he says, "You don't order your tools, they accumulate. You find them; you use them and they follow you." He illustrates by showing how a piece of dry bark will make a pattern when it is pressed into a moist clay tile or the walls of a pot. The tool may also be a button, a metal cap from a jam jar, a handfull of coarse sawdust from a carpenter's rip saw. The texture photographs in this book indicate only a few of the limitless surface patterns the imaginative potter can create with "found" tools.

In a typical demonstration of surface ornamentation for a class, Carlton Ball places six layers of newspaper on a table or the floor. Then he empties a bowl of thick, heavily grogged clay slip into a small bag, the kind pastry cooks use for decorating cakes. He squeezes heavy slip on the top sheet of paper, creating a pattern of a line of short turns and wide sweeping curves. Then he lifts a still moist clay lamp base and gently lays one side down on the clay slip. Much of the slip clings to the side of the lamp. Slip is then squeezed onto a fresh piece of paper and another side of the lamp gets the treatment. By the time the fourth side of the lamp has received its pattern of slip, the students feel the muscles of their hands and arms moving in concert with the new skills being demonstrated.

In teaching by demonstration, Carlton Ball says little. Talk isn't necessary. Every gesture is articulate. He prefers the excellent old method of teaching by example rather than wordy precept or class lecture. Thus, in this book, the author guides the reader with visual demonstrations, showing each of the major steps in texturing and forming in clear detail.

There are many who buy instruction books for the graphic directions they contain. One of the visual ideas is borrowed and work begins. It may soon become apparent, however, that the result is straying from the original idea presented in the book. One should not stop, but go right on. The new interpretation will be better — and more personal.

With this book you are able to work alone, with no one to hinder by offering advice or asking, "What are you doing, anyway?" Be thankful that you are so privileged. Working alone intensifies individuality. The finished piece may not turn out as originally hoped, for during the creative act the imagination does not always consider the details that the eye picks up after the work is finished. After a day or two when the work is seen with a fresh eye, however, its originality will be apparent.

A single idea may prevail in the beginning; yet ideas, like knowledge, are cumulative. They combine and grow. Then the clay works even more willingly.

Glen Lukens
Los Angeles

INTRODUCTION

CLAY

Clay is the most elemental of materials and one of the most useful. It may be as close at hand as your own doorstep, for nearly a quarter of the earth is composed of clay and clay-making materials. You may find it in creek beds, lake beds, along the banks of rivers and in fields. Nature is in a continual process of producing clay in great quantities.

Over the centuries man has devised many uses for this versatile plastic material — from containers for food to houses for shelter. Indeed, clay artifacts, sometimes thousands of years old, have given modern archaeologists a remarkably accurate key to the study of ancient civilizations.

Knowledge of ways to utilize clay has increased with time. Today clay-like materials are used to form parts of rockets which traverse outer space. Yet, even after centuries of working with clay, there are still questions to be answered. There is an excitement in the interaction of clay and fire that continues to fascinate man, inviting him to experiment, to discover ever new uses and mysterious qualities.

In working with clay you may also discover things about yourself. It may touch off sparks of latent creative talent, causing you to produce pieces as interesting as those made by craftsmen who lived thousands of years before you. It is the aim of this book to help you become aware of and develop these creative senses and to become a worthy craftsman.

TEXTURES

Creating something useful with your own hands is a basic urge, and the desire to mark into wet, unblemished surfaces is instinctive with all of us. Almost everyone can recall times when he has been tempted to touch wet paint — to make *certain* it was wet — or to inscribe names and initials into wet cement. Small wonder that potters working with wet, impressionable clay frequently carve into or scratch its surface, build it up or polish it to change the texture or give it a different character.

Clay is so sensitive that it always bears the stamp of the potter's own personality. Designs are so easily impressed into its yielding surface that the ways and means of texturing are limited only by the artist's imagination. To stimulate the imagination he must learn to *see* as well as look and thus reach beyond the mere recognition of objects. When he has gained a little creative insight, the chance observation of foot prints in wet sand or even automobile tire tracks will take on new meaning and suggest patterns. His inspiration can start from observing a motif as majestic as the escarpments of the Grand Canyon or by handling an object as humble as the bobbin of a sewing machine.

Texturing clay has been dealt with in great detail. You will find it fun to work in this manner, and it will stimulate your imagination. Textures can be extremely handsome if used with restraint and good taste.

Texturing pottery, especially hand-built pottery, is also practical, for it covers the imperfections of hand work. The process strengthens the joints as well as covers them. The tool marks are an honest result of the construction. They are valid and add character.

HAND FORMING

Anyone who has watched an expert potter throw forms on the wheel has had the urge to try it. It is intriguing to watch the clay take shape. It appears to be so simple, so much *fun*! This appearance, however, is deceiving. It takes much practice to learn to control clay on a potter's wheel. It is an acquired skill comparable to playing the piano. A potter's wheel is also a large investment for a beginner. A good deal of space is required to house it, and it is not easy to move about. In addition, pieces made on the wheel are limited to symmetrical shapes.

The flexibility of hand-forming, on the other hand, offers endless opportunities for shapes that cannot be produced on the potter's wheel. A beginner can be successful almost immediately and learn to express himself in a very individual way when making pieces by hand. The tools are simple and inexpensive. A special workshop or studio is not needed to produce a beautiful piece of pottery. The only requirement is a table in your kitchen, garage or back porch on which to do the work. Hand-forming is an intimate concept that includes only the clay, the hands of the potter and the potter's own ideas.

This book offers a complete compilation of all the basic techniques of forming useful objects of clay without using a potter's wheel. It will save the potter hours of time hunting through books and innumerable magazines to find the various techniques he wants. It should be pointed out, however, that *this is not a beginning book on pottery*, nor is it a survey of hand-building. It is a study-in-depth of a limited but important area in ceramics.

The Glossary of Terms and the opening pages of Chapter 16 were written as a special guide for the beginner, but he should supplement these with an elementary book on pottery or prepare himself with a beginning course in pottery. In either way he can acquire a working knowledge of the basic terms and techniques.

The techniques illustrated in the following chapters start with simple projects suitable for elementary school children and progress to those of considerable difficulty. The emphasis is on simple, direct ways of working that will encourage the beginner rather than defeat him by showing at the outset involved techniques and difficult pieces to form. Every piece illustrated in this book was designed, made and photographed by Mr. Ball to show the relationship of form and texture.

FINISHES

Both the shape and the purpose of the piece should determine which color and finish to select. If the piece is delicate in design, it obviously calls for a treatment different from that to be used on a large primitive-type piece designed, perhaps, for use out-of-doors. In the latter instance, weather and the surrounding landscape should also be taken into consideration.

The final steps of finishing and glazing add color and character to what has been made. The selection of both should be carefully considered and, like the successful merging of texture and form, *should become one* with the other elements in pottery-making.

The last chapters in this book set forth suggestions for the finishing of pottery, firing, the selection of glazes and a variety of recipes for glazes and colors.

Don't be discouraged by not having a pottery studio in which to work. Unprofessional surroundings, a limited number of tools and no professional equipment may well be an advantage in calling forth your ingenuity. The examples shown in this book, which were made in a kitchen, are distinct from those made in a classroom. The environment in which they were made has influenced the work and given it a special character.

It is important to be alert and let your physical surroundings influence your activities because this will make each effort a creative one and give it individuality. Every potter will produce something that is distinctly his own without consciously trying because of *where he works* and *what he selects to work with*.

Something mysterious happens between the clay and an honest workman, and when it does, an original and handsome creation takes form.

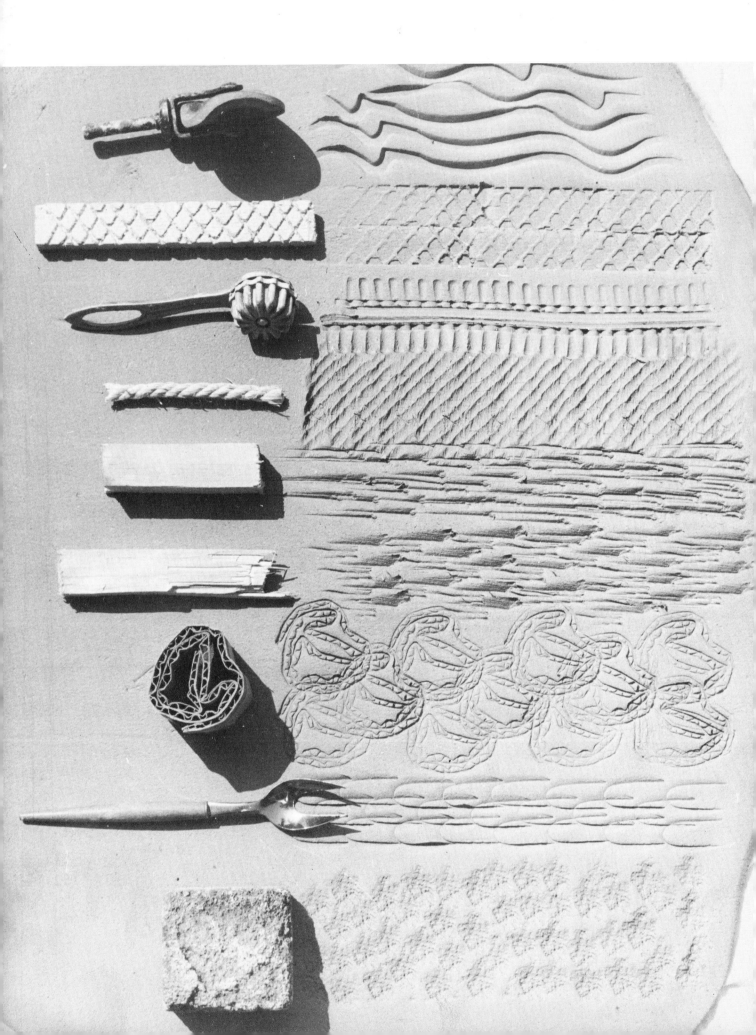

FIGURE 1. Almost any tool can make interesting textures.

1. TEXTURING CLAY

Primitive man first experimented with textures by pressing wet clay into baskets, thereby producing a woven pattern on the outsides of his pots. Later, he incised clay with whatever tools or implements were at hand. The technique of rolling a pattern into clay is as old as pottery itself. Outstanding examples are found in the cuneiform writing of the ancient Babylonians, Assyrians and Persians. The early Chinese and Europeans and the Indians of pre-Columbian South America used this technique to decorate pots. The textured pottery left by these ancient craftsmen has enabled us to learn much of their history and to gain a wide knowledge of the early culture of man. For today's creative potter the value of studying the arts and techniques of past cultures lies not in copying them but in the inspiration he finds for new applications of ancient ideas.

Some ceramics seem to ask for texture to enrich and unify them. The texture can be delicate and fine or bold and deep. It may be scattered and abstract, rhythmical or asymmetrical. It can be a repeat pattern or a single motif. But whichever technique is subscribed to, the resulting pattern should be indigenous to the clay itself and enhance the form.

When developing ideas for new textures, let the clay speak for itself. Any attempt to imitate driftwood, marble or other surfaces foreign to the true nature of clay will look false.

To begin exploring the endless possibilities of texturing you must start with a clay surface that is not too wet, nor yet too dry. A bit of experimenting will tell you exactly when it feels right for your purpose.

You might start by spreading a dry dish towel or a section of old sheeting on a table. Then, place a lump of clay on the cloth and pound it into a large, thick pancake. With a rolling pin make it about three-eighths inch thick.

Your fingers are your best tools, so try them first. Make regular imprints with your fingertips. Then try dragging your fingertips as they press into the clay. Also try pinching a bit of clay into a mound and twisting it slightly. Repeat these marks regularly. There are many other patterns that can be made with the fingers.

You can press objects into the clay to create a repeat pattern. Look inside a woman's purse. A lipstick tube, an eyebrow pencil, a thimble or compact will produce a variety of designs, and a comb pulled through the clay will work wonders. Even your fingernail will create a number of good textures.

FIGURE 2. Clay pressed with the index finger into an evenly spaced pattern.

FIGURE 3. Fingertip depressions alternately spaced.

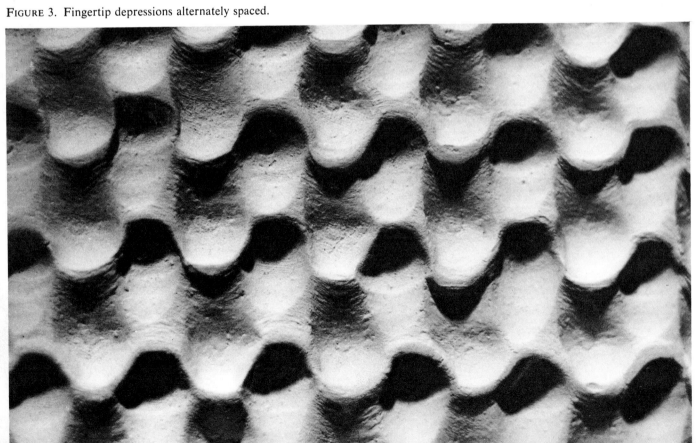

Go through a man's pockets. Here you may find a knife, keys, coins, pencil or pen and numerous other items that suggest texturing. The kitchen drawers will yield a generous supply of texturing tools. So will a child's toy box. Visit a hardware store or gourmet shop. The sources for usable items are inexhaustible.

Press the objects into clay or drag them through the surface to obtain unusual patterns. For an overall design, roll clay out on a piece of heavily textured fabric such as burlap or monk's cloth.

Here is a brief list of tools you might use to make textures in clay:

Fancy paring knives	Ravioli cutter
Apple corer	Toy automobile wheels
Pie-edge crimper	Shells of nuts
Serving fork	Sea shells
Swedish rolling pin used for flatbread	Broken piece of cement
	Scissors handles
Rolled-up piece of leather	Twigs from trees
	Dicers and choppers
Handle of a spoon	Seed pods
Plastic screw-on tops	Dry breakfast cereals
Children's construction blocks	rolled in a cloth
	Dog grooming combs

There are many pottery techniques that lend themselves to using pre-textured clay, while others require that the structure be built first, with the texturing added as a final embellishment. Both methods have a place in creating pottery forms.

It is a good idea to explore texturing first by rolling out many sheets of clay in uniform sizes. You can control the thickness by measuring the sides with a stick. The entire family can be drafted into such a project and enjoy it, or a group of friends can have fun making practice textured sheets, which, when completed, can be formed into tiles or "hot pads," or combined to make an attractive tabletop. With a sufficient number of tiles you can add interest to a patio floor or entryway. Tiles can also be used to create wall panels for patio or garden.

To make textured tiles, begin by cutting out a simple cardboard pattern, determining beforehand the shape and size you want. Modules in various sizes will work well. They could be, for example, 2 x 2, 2 x 4, 4 x 6 inches, and so on. Trace around the cardboard patterns and cut out the textured clay panels (Figure 38).

Here is another project for the entire family: With red, buff and white clays and blends of these colors, make clay marbles of all sizes. Flatten them out into round or oval shapes. Some or all of the shapes may be textured. After they have been fired, these pieces can be used in a mosaic technique for a handsome tabletop, wall panel or floor area (Figure 39).

For a more complex tile form, cut out simple silhouettes of objects and apply texture. You might cut out a variety of fish shapes, then texture them to simulate scales and fins. The fish forms can be glued to a fabric such as heavy linen to create an unusual wall panel (Figure 40). The forms might also be combined with tesserae to make a striking mosaic, or glued to a garden or patio wall with epoxy cement.

We are surrounded by a wealth of usable objects of which only a few have been mentioned. Have the fun of discovering for yourself new texturing tools and trying various ways in which to use them creatively.

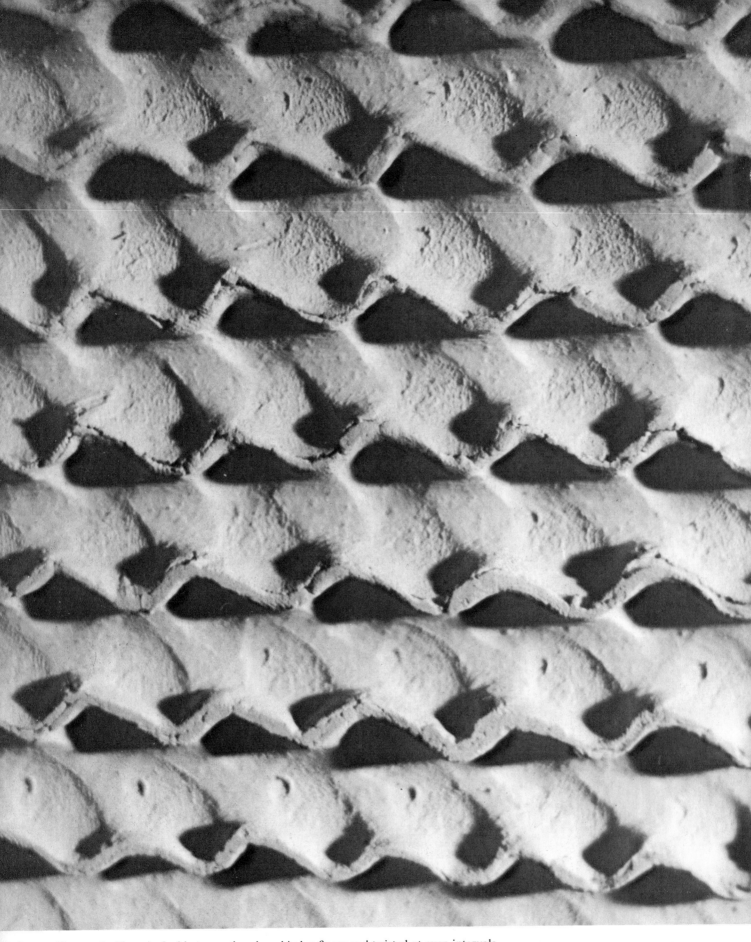

FIGURE 4. Clay pinched between thumb and index finger and twisted at even intervals.

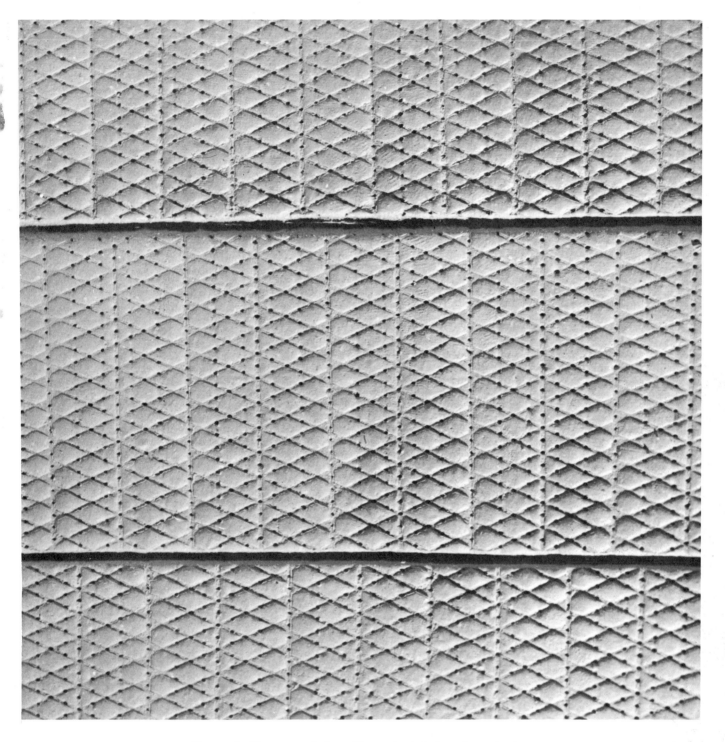

FIGURE 5. Texture made by rolling a plastic hair curler onto clay.

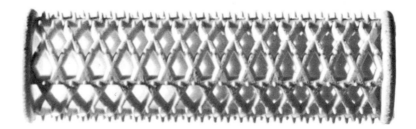

17

FIGURE 6. A short length of rope rolled onto clay.

18

FIGURE 7. Broken end of a wooden stick slapped onto a clay surface.

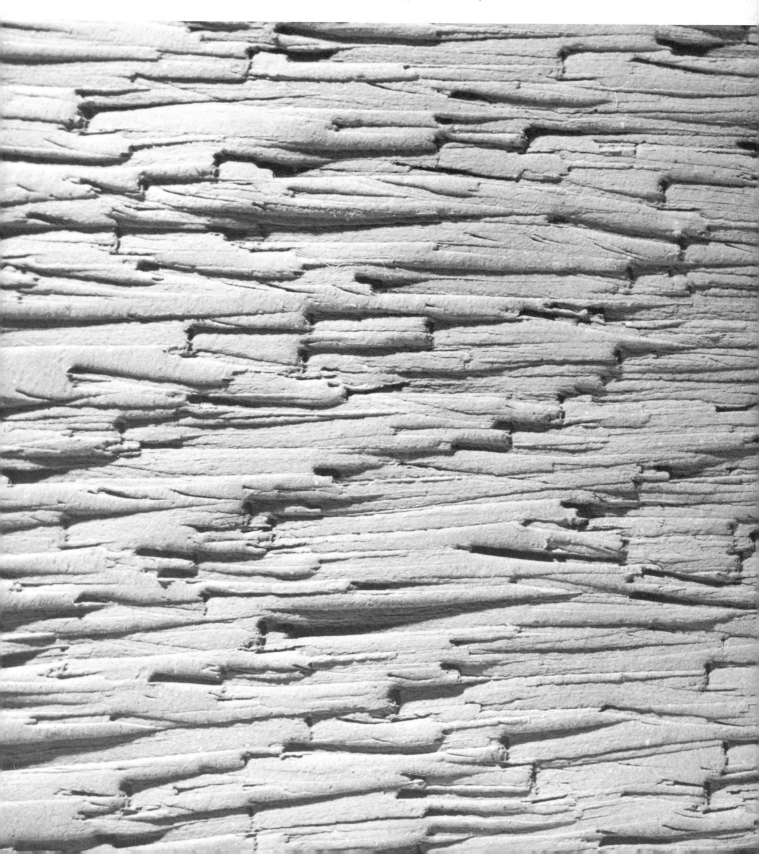

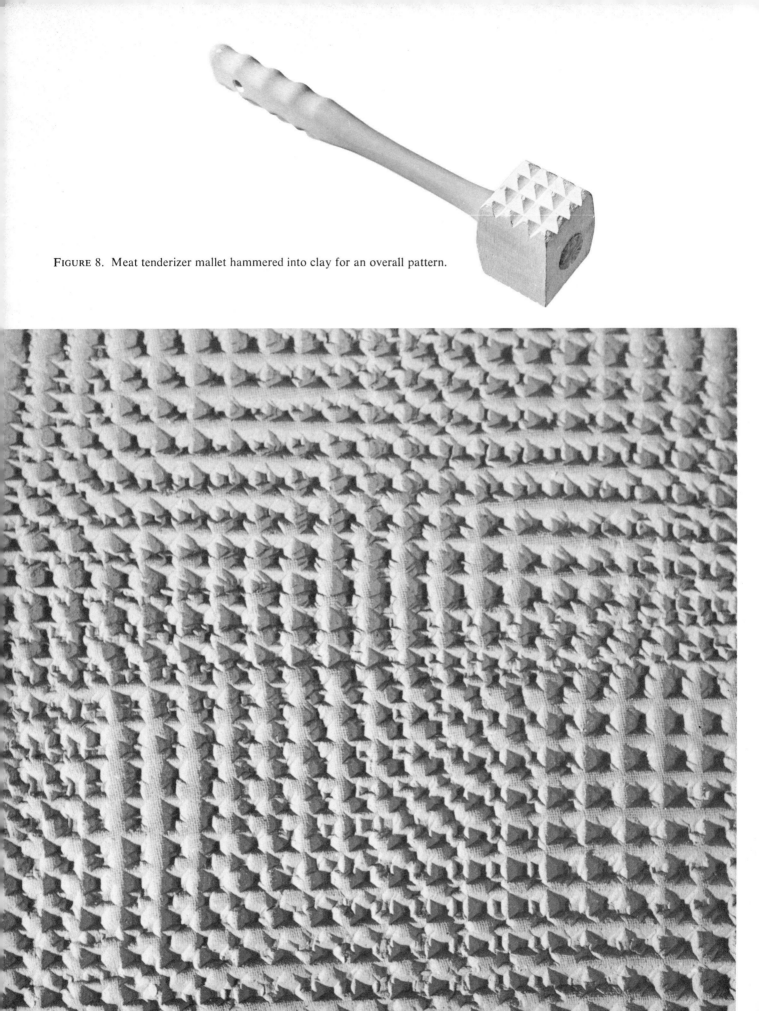

FIGURE 8. Meat tenderizer mallet hammered into clay for an overall pattern.

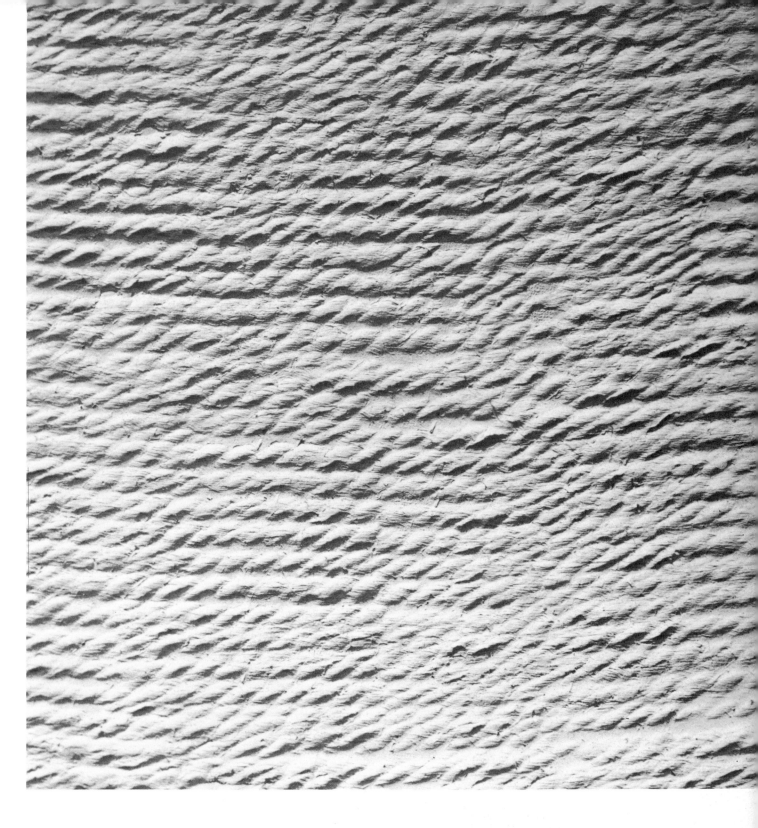

FIGURE 9. Cord wrapped around a stick makes a paddle for texturing clay.

FIGURE 10. Edge and corner of a wooden stick paddled into clay.

FIGURE 11. Piece of rough tree bark pressed into clay.

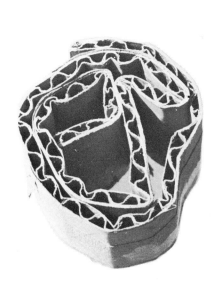

FIGURE 12. Rolled-up strip of corrugated cardboard stippled onto clay.

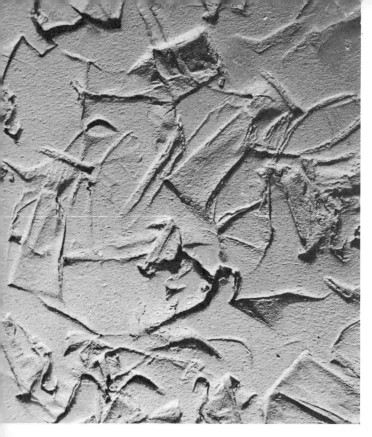

FIGURE 13. Small aluminum pie tin crumpled and stippled onto clay.

FIGURE 14. A wooden stick cross-hatched with a saw blade makes a texturing paddle.

24

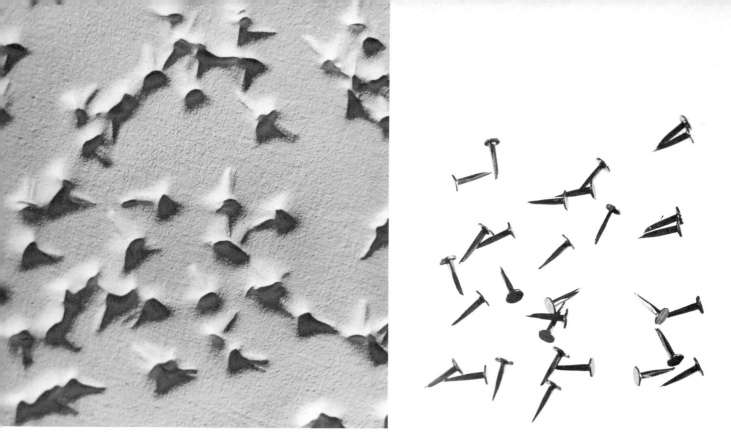

FIGURE 15. Clay pressed over carpet tacks covered with a piece of cloth.

FIGURE 16. A fragment of broken brick used to stipple the clay.

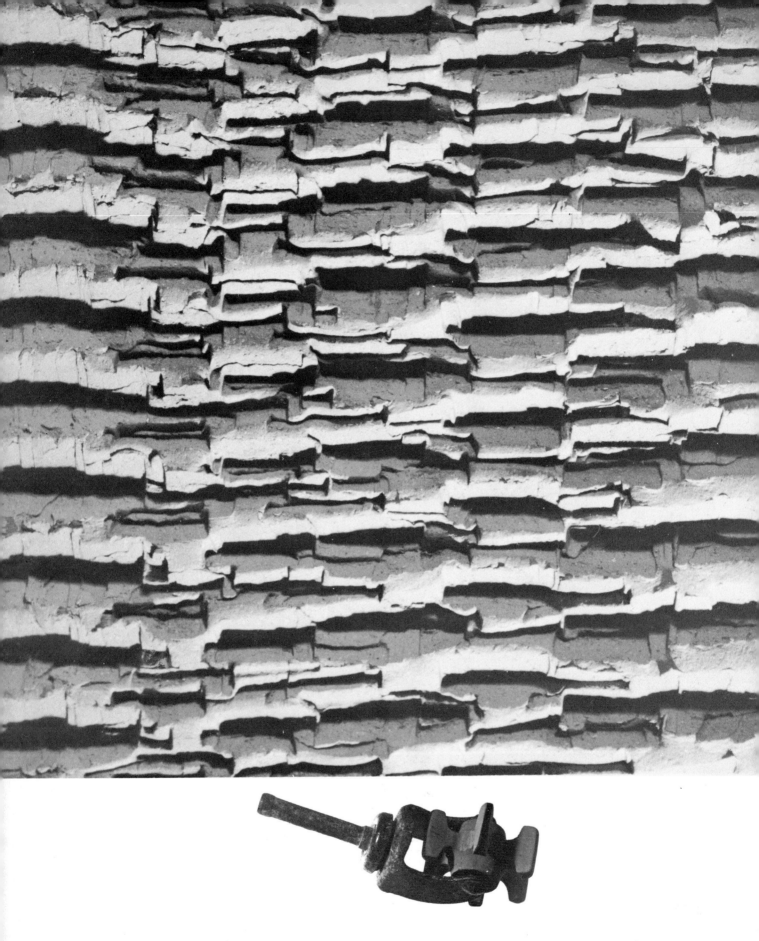

Figure 17. Plaster furniture caster, carved to emulate a Mexican spur, repeatedly rolled into clay.

26

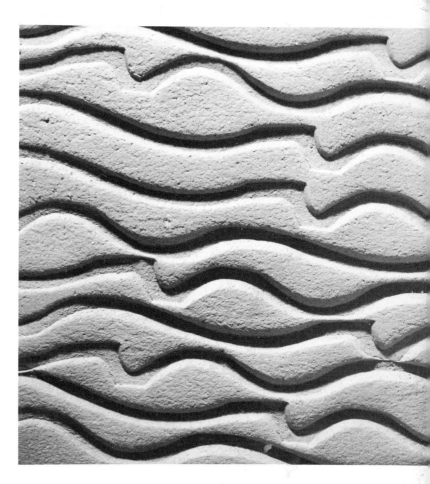

FIGURE 18. Carved plastic furniture caster rolled into clay.

FIGURE 19. A slice of wooden rolling pin was filed into a pattern and rolled into the clay with a wire coat-hanger handle.

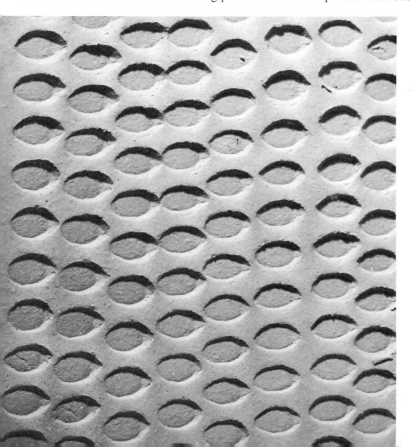

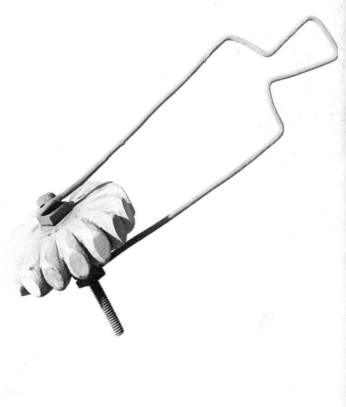

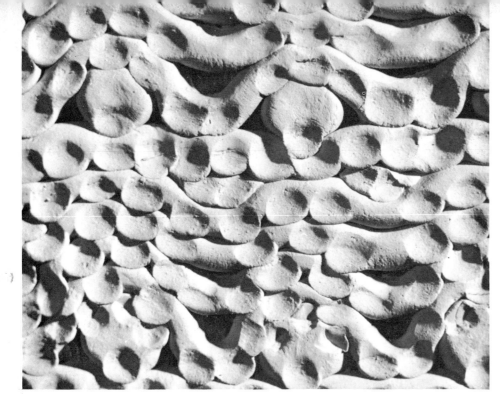

FIGURE 20. Clay coils pressed together with the fingers create an interesting surface.

FIGURE 21. Variation of clay coils pressed together with fingers.

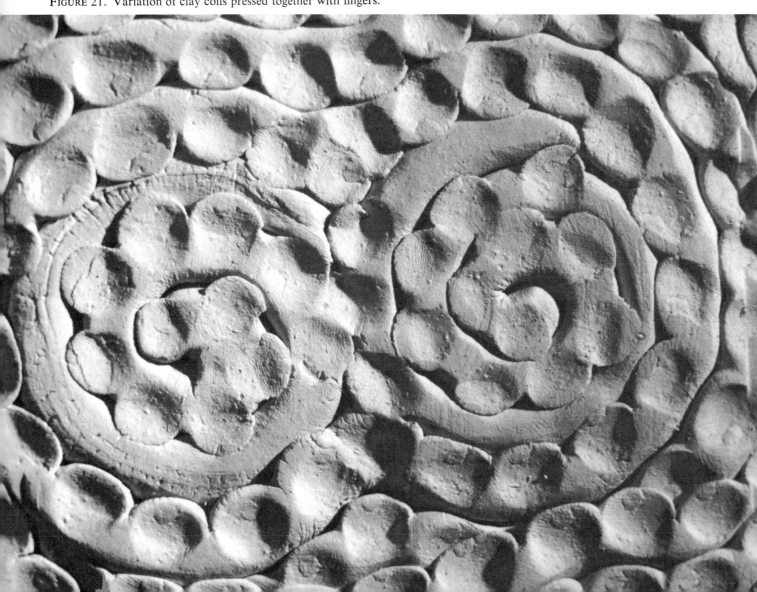

FIGURE 22. The edge of a ruler pressed into clay.

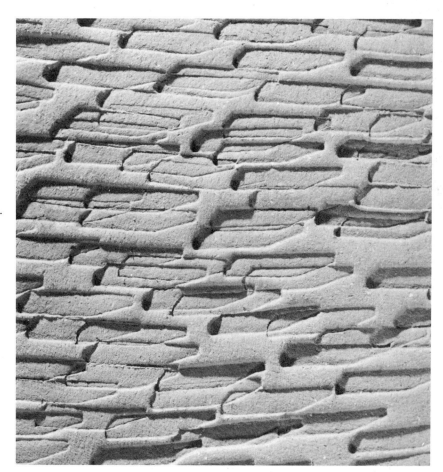

FIGURE 23. The end of a ruler pressed into clay.

29

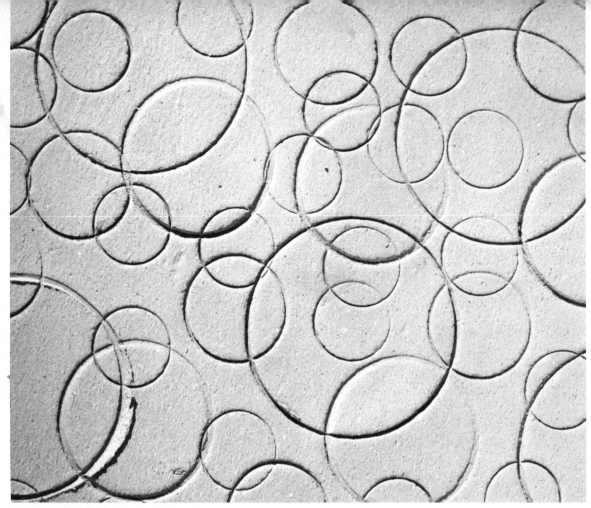

FIGURE 24. Jar tops pressed into clay.

FIGURE 25. String pressed into clay.

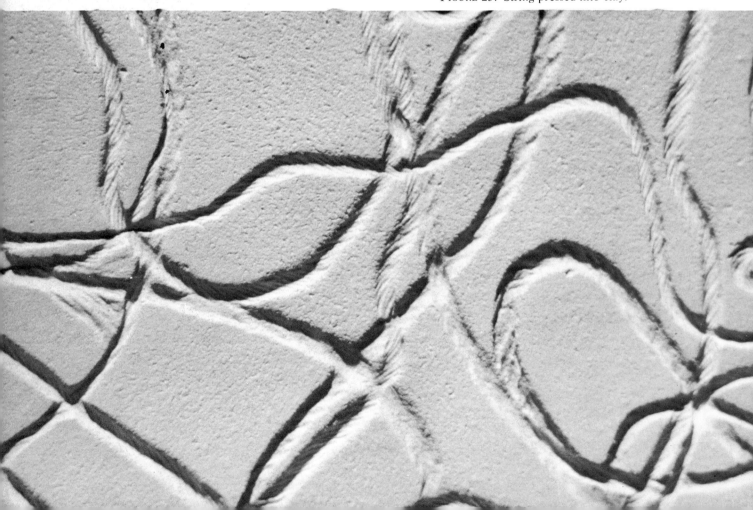

FIGURE 26. Indented Styrofoam pressed into clay.

FIGURE 27. Piece of dry sponge pressed into clay.

FIGURE 28. Indented Styrofoam pressed into clay.

FIGURE 29. Clay rolled onto knitted nylon.

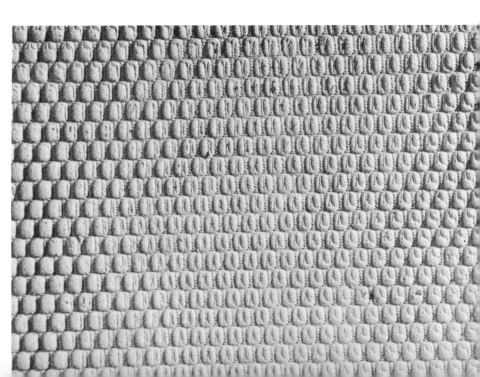

FIGURE 30. Indented Styrofoam pressed into clay.

FIGURE 31. Clay rolled onto expanded metal lath.

FIGURE 32. Stick cut with saw blade paddled into clay.

FIGURE 33. Clay pressed onto ordinary household straw broom.

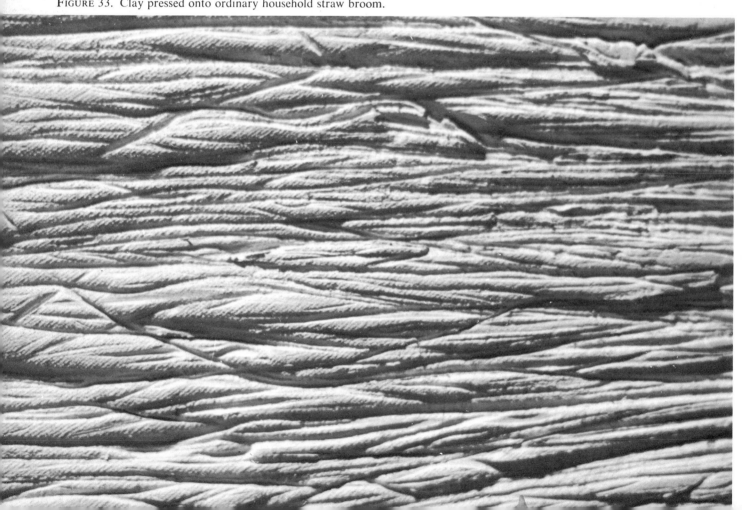

Figure 34. Clay rolled out on burlap.

FIGURE 36. Kitchen door spring stretched and pulled through clay.

FIGURE 35. Carved furniture caster rolled into clay.

FIGURE 37. Carved furniture caster rolled into clay.

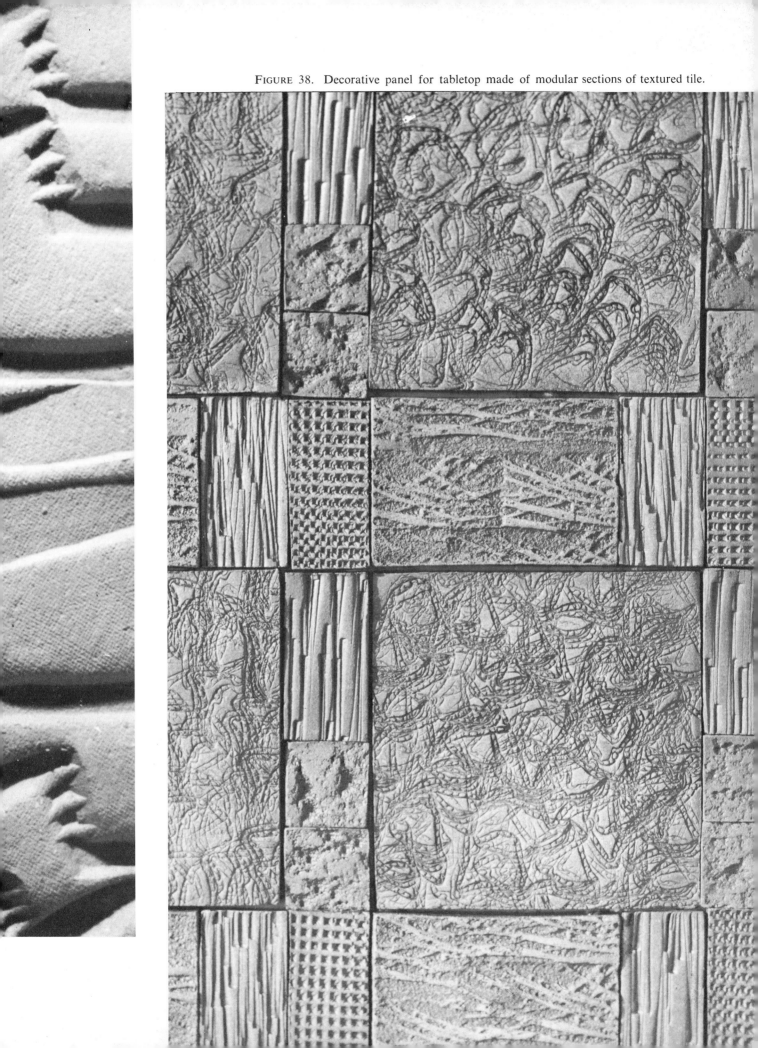

FIGURE 38. Decorative panel for tabletop made of modular sections of textured tile.

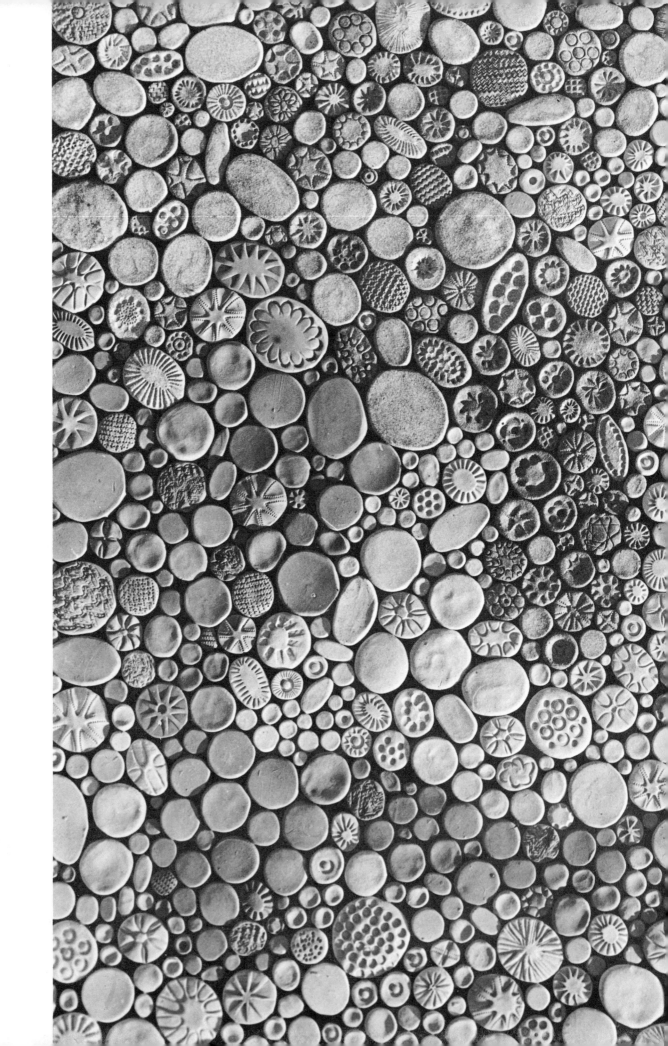

FIGURE 39. Clay marbles of various colors, flattened and textured, are mounted in a mosaic technique for a wall panel or tabletop.

FIGURE 40. Fish silhouettes cut from clay, textured and cemented to a fabric-covered board for a wall panel.

FIGURE 41. The technique for forming this simple fish platter is the same as that used for the leaf platter described in this chapter. Finished in a glaze of your own choice, this platter could be used for baking or serving. It makes an excellent dish for serving Japanese food or for serving food around a swimming pool.

2. DRAPING CLAY INTO A CLAY MOLD

Draping clay into a clay mold is a direct and extremely simple technique for producing original pottery forms. It is especially good for beginners in ceramics because it leads the student easily from his experience in drawing, or two-dimensional design, to three-dimensional concepts in art. For the more experienced potter, it is yet another way to stimulate the imagination toward creative work.

The forming process is as follows: Make a small sketch — several if necessary — the actual size you want the clay piece to be when finished. Cut out the paper shape with a pair of scissors. Then spread a dish towel over a drawing board.

Take a suitable lump of clay and pat it into a large, thick pancake on the dish towel. With a rolling pin, roll over the clay in several directions until it is one-quarter inch thick for small objects or three-eighths inch for larger containers.

When the clay slab is rolled thin enough and is smooth, place the cut-out paper pattern on top of it. Trace around it lightly. If details are drawn on the paper pattern, transfer them to the clay by tracing over the lines with a pencil. The pressure of the pencil point will make a depression in the clay.

The paper pattern used to make the leaf-shaped dish shown in Figure 46 began as a simple oval shape. You can make such a dish in the following manner (Figures 42 through 46):

After the shape has been traced onto the clay, cut the clay into a rough oval that starts approximately one inch outside the traced pattern. Remove excess clay from the slab.

The next step is to apply the incised design, using a square wooden stick as a tool. First make the two lines that form the stem of the leaf. Press the corner of the stick firmly into the clay to produce the V-shaped lines. Make the veins on the leaf by placing the end of the stick, on a diagonal, next to the central vein and pressing the corner of the stick firmly into the clay. The leaf shape can be cut out with a needle fastened to the end of a wooden dowel.

It is now time to make the mold. Roll out a coil of clay about an inch in diameter and curve it into an oval the size of the paper pattern. Trim the ends and join them smoothly. Transfer the one-inch, oval-shaped coil of clay to a board for support and easy handling. Lay strips of paper toweling over the coil to keep it from becoming sticky. The mold is then complete.

The last step in construction is to drape the clay over the mold. To do this you must slide one hand gently under the cloth on which the clay leaf is resting. Place the other hand on top of the clay and flip the leaf over. Now peel the cloth off the leaf. Flip the clay leaf right-side-up again, and lay it over the coil of clay. Then gently force the leaf down into the clay mold to obtain the form you want, pressing it deep enough so that the bottom lies *flat* on the table. When the dish is firm and easy to handle, trim it if necessary or sponge the edges to give it a nice finish. After the dish has dried thoroughly, remove it from the mold and it is ready for the bisque fire.

After you have made a simple dish with this method, you should be ready to try more complicated forms such as the fish platter shown in Figure 41. It was made by the same forming technique.

A variation of this technique for making a rectan-gular shallow plate is illustrated in Figures 47 through 50. Instead of using a round coil for the mold, which, of course, could also be done, roll out a thick slab of clay onto a piece of cloth. Cut a rectangle out of the clay slab. Then cut another, smaller, rectangle out of the center of the first rectangle, and the clay mold is made. Lay strips of paper toweling over the clay rectangle to prevent its sticking to the piece to be formed.

Next roll out a thinner slab of clay onto another piece of cloth. Put texture on part of this thin slab. Place a rectangular paper pattern on top of the clay slab and cut the clay to shape with a steel needle. Then drape the textured slab of clay over the clay mold, just as you did in making the leaf-shaped dish.

After the rectangular slab of clay is pressed down into the mold and the shaping is finished, set it aside to dry. When it is dry, it can be removed from the mold, and it is ready for bisque firing.

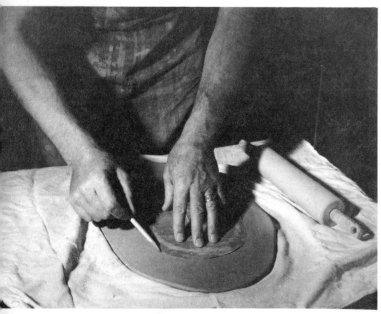

FIGURE 42. Tracing around the oval paper pattern on a sheet of clay three-eighths inch thick. Point and stem are added to make a leaf silhouette.

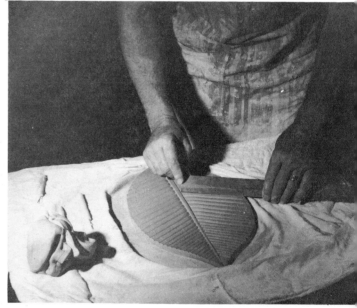

FIGURE 43. The edge or corner of a wooden stick or a ruler is pressed into the clay to make a V-shaped depression. This is repeated to make the desired design.

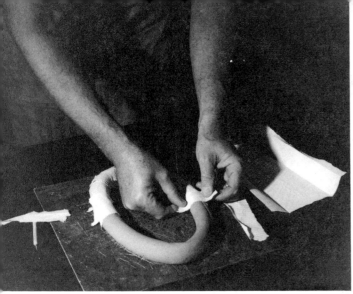

FIGURE 44. A one-inch coil of clay is rolled out and bent into an oval shape the size of the paper pattern. The clay is covered with strips of paper towel or newspaper.

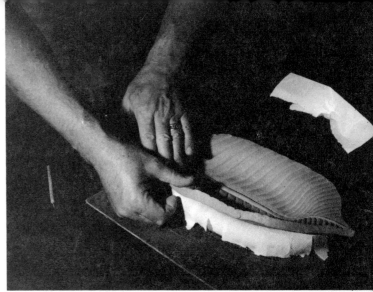

FIGURE 45. Draping the clay leaf over the oval-shaped coil of clay. The leaf is pressed gently into the mold to give it the desired shape.

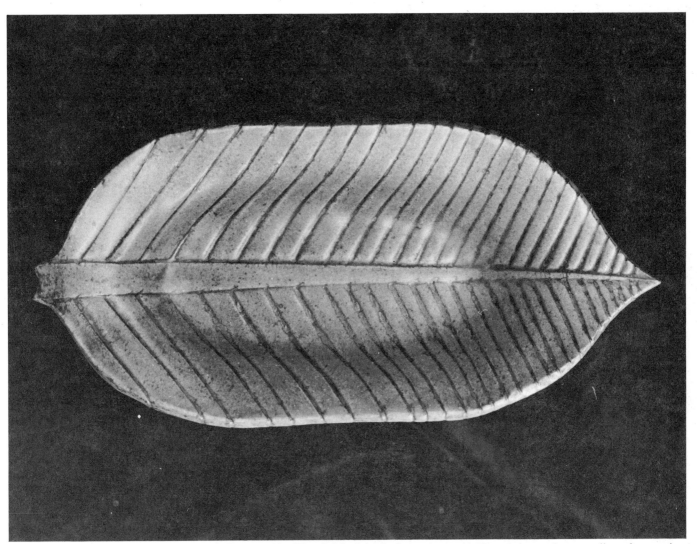

FIGURE 46. The finished leaf platter is practical and decorative, excellent for serving food. A variety of leaf-shaped platters would be effective for use at a Hawaiian luau. The bisque leaf was stained with iron oxide, then sponged to leave iron in the depressions. A Chun Celadon glaze was sprayed on, then fired to cone 10 in a reduction atmosphere.

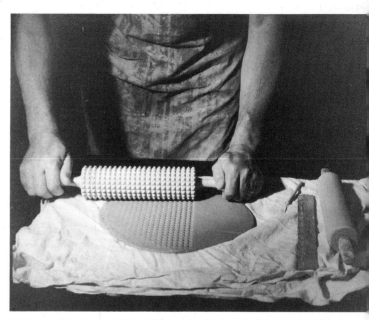

FIGURE 47. To make one type of rectangular clay mold, a thick slab of clay is rolled out and cut into a hollow rectangle. The width of the clay mold determines the width of the rim of the platter.

FIGURE 48. A Swedish rolling pin designed for making flatbread (purchased from a gourmet shop) is used to texture the second, thinner sheet of clay.

FIGURE 49. A rectangle is cut from the sheet of textured clay. It should be about the size of the clay mold. The textured rectangle is placed over the mold and pressed into the mold to shape it as desired.

FIGURE 50. The finished rectangular platter. The textured area is glazed with Green Brown G Mat 3 glaze. It was fired to cone 10 in a reduction atmosphere.

FIGURE 51. Wall vase made by draping clay over a newspaper mold. There are many variations on the basic piece that are exciting and beautiful.

3. DRAPING CLAY OVER A NEWSPAPER MOLD

A simple way to make a wall planter or a vase is to drape clay over a newspaper core. Here are the first basic steps:

1. Roll out a good-size sheet of clay, three-eighths inch thick, on a dish towel.

2. Place several sheets of newspaper over the clay slab.

3. Put a drawing board on top of the paper and flip clay, paper and board over.

4. Peel the dish towel off the clay.

5. Apply some interesting textures to the clay.

Now (Figures 52 through 55), from part of the clay slab cut an oval shape. It need not be perfect. Crumple a sheet of newspaper into a loose ball. Place this just below the center of the textured clay oval.

Cut out a smaller half-oval from the remainder of the textured clay slab, and place it over the crumpled ball of newspaper. Gently bend the curved edges down over the paper until they touch the bottom slab of clay. Pinch the edges of this clay onto the bottom slab. In order to make good seams, you must be thorough. Punch one or two holes near the top of the large, flat clay slab so that the finished planter may be fastened to a wall. Now the forming is completed, and the piece should be allowed to dry.

The newspaper can remain inside the smaller half-oval. It becomes moist and soft on exposure to the clay, and, because the clay shrinks as it dries, the soft paper ball compresses. In the bisque fire the paper will burn up without affecting the clay piece.

The fired container may be fastened to a patio, garage or garden wall. It can also be hung on a fence, or indoors. It will serve as either a planter or a vase and can be made decorative simply by filling it with water and planting a sweet potato that will sprout into delicate, trailing vines.

There are innumerable single or multiple shapes that can be made in this way. If the container is filled with soil and peat moss and then planted with various succulents, it will remain beautiful the year round.

49

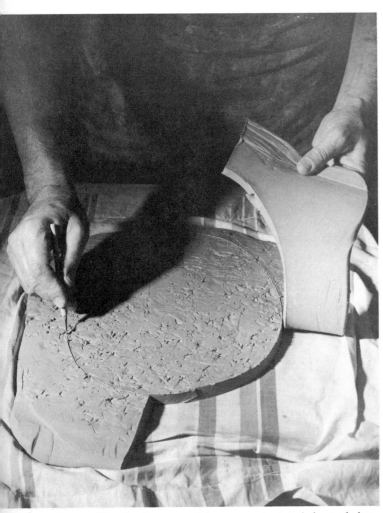 

FIGURE 52. Cutting an oval from a pre-textured sheet of clay. The texture shown here was applied with a crumpled ball of wrapping paper.

FIGURE 53. Placing a clay half-oval over a ball of crumpled newspaper on the large oval slab of clay.

FIGURE 54. The clay is pressed gently over the newspaper and stretched into shape. The edges are pinched onto the bottom clay slab.

FIGURE 55. The finished wall vase or wall planter. The texture was stained with Barnard Clay slip applied to the bisque clay. The glaze was PM5 Eggshell Tan, poured into and over the stained bisque ware, then fired to cone 10 in a reduction atmosphere.

FIGURE 56. An unusual pot made by folding clay over a newspaper mold; it was textured with the edge of a book of paper matches. The form was turned over to add the two feet, and the necks were connected to complete the form. Blue-green Waxy glaze was used on the neck, then fired to cone 10 in a reduction atmosphere. Barnard Clay slip was used on the biscuit to stain the body of the vase.

4. FOLDING CLAY OVER A NEWSPAPER MOLD

This is a simple yet effective technique for forming some types of pottery. Anyone who has ever made meat pies, Mexican tacos or apple turnovers should be able to apply these comparable cooking techniques to making clay forms of this variety.

Begin by cutting a long, narrow oval pattern from a piece of paper. To do this, fold a sheet of paper over twice and cut a quarter-arch out of the folded right angle of the paper. Unfold the paper. If the resulting oval shape needs further shaping, refold the paper and trim it again. After the paper pattern is made, the actual forming begins (Figures 57 through 65).

First, roll out a long, narrow sheet of clay about three-eighths inch thick. Place the paper pattern on top of the clay. With a needle, cut the clay into an oval following the pattern.

Now roll out a coil of clay about one inch thick and place it along the edge of the oval, and extending about half-way around it. Pinch the edges together on the bottom side.

Next take a sheet of newspaper and crumple it into a wad. This is your filling, or newspaper mold. Put it on the lower half of the oval where the one-inch coil is welded into place. Then fold over the top half of the oval piece of clay so that the edges of the clay rest on the *top part* of the coil. Weld these edges together. Now the newspaper is concealed inside the clay form. If the form does not have much volume, blow it up.

To do this put a "marble" of clay on the form and weld it in place. Punch a hole through the clay marble and the clay slab with a pencil. With your mouth, blow air into the clay piece. It will puff up, even burst a seam if you blow too hard. If a seam opens up, patch it and blow the form up again. Then pinch the hole shut with your teeth and lips to trap air in the form. This will help the wet clay keep its shape. Plug the hole and smooth over this area.

Now with a stick, paddle the clay into the shape you desire; then let it stand until it becomes stiff enough to hold its own shape.

You are now ready to texture the clay in the way you feel will be the most effective. In the illustrations one form was paddled with the edge of an enamel bowl. The other was stamped with the edge of a book of paper matches (Figures 65 and 56).

Now you must decide on the final form. First, study the piece closely right-side-up, then turn the other end up. What kind of neck, or opening, and foot would be best suited to the piece? There are many ways to finish the form to give it character. The form lends itself to a hanging bottle with one, two or three spouts, or two spouts and a handle. Sketch several ideas before you decide on the finish.

The vase in the step-by-step illustrations had a foot added with straps of clay that were pre-formed by curving them over a rolling pin. When the foot is added, the seams must be carefully welded; otherwise they will crack open. The folded part of the form — the *wide* part — was textured with the edge of a square stick.

Thirteen small necks were added to the top in this simple manner: Clay marbles were made, then pinched into tapering solid cylinders. These clay cylinders were carefully attached to the top of the vase. When the clay was firm enough to hold its own shape, holes were punched into the form by pushing a pencil through the center of each neck. If the clay is wet when the holes are punched and the air pressure is eliminated, the form may collapse. If the clay becomes too dry before the holes are punched, the air pressure increases and the clay shrinks, causing the form to crack.

Round off the edges of the punched holes and let the vase dry so it can be bisque fired. The newspaper filling, or mold, will burn up in the firing with no damage to the vase.

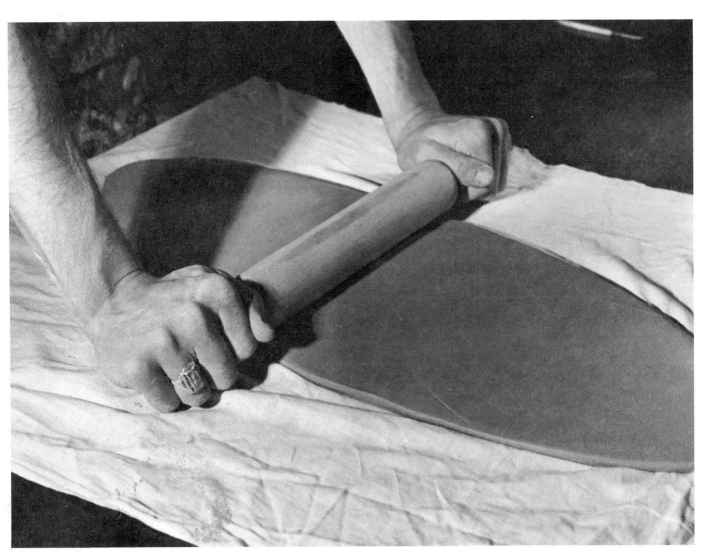

FIGURE 57. Rolling out a long, narrow sheet of clay about three-eighths inch thick.

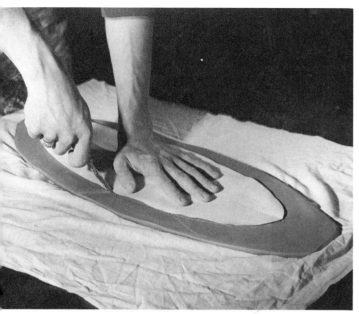

FIGURE 58. Cutting out a long, narrow oval, using a paper pattern as guide.

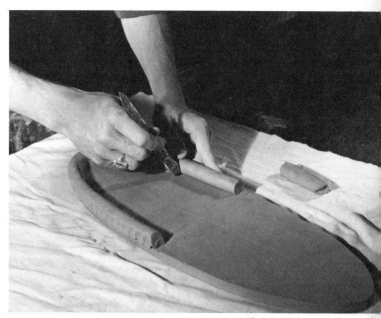

FIGURE 59. A one-inch coil of clay is placed around the edge of one-half the clay oval. The edges are pinched together.

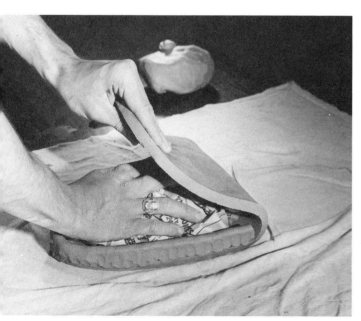

FIGURE 60. A wad of newspaper is placed on the bottom half of the clay oval and the top half is folded over it.

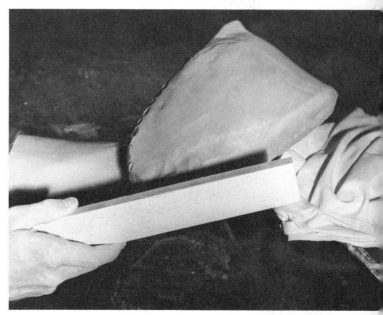

FIGURE 61. Welding the seams together and paddling the form into shape.

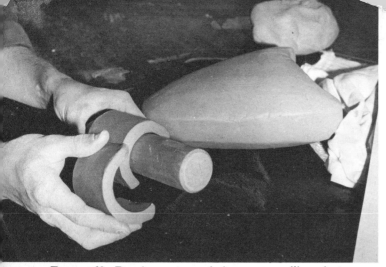

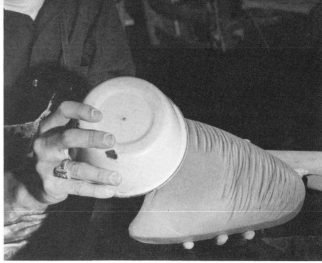

FIGURE 62. Draping a strap of clay over a rolling pin to pre-form the base.

FIGURE 63. Texturing the form with the edge of a bowl.

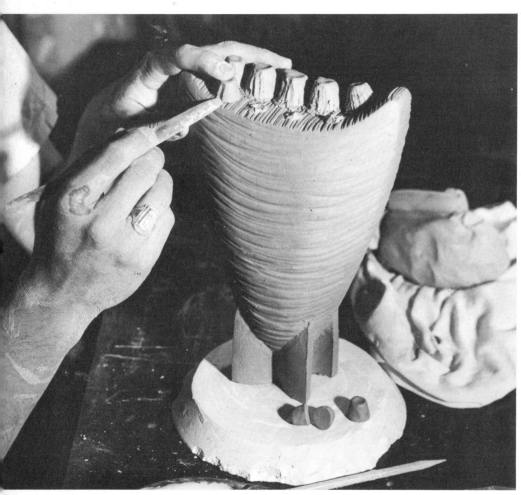

FIGURE 64. Solid wads of clay are applied to the top of the piece to form spouts. When the clay is firm enough to hold its shape, holes are punched in the spouts and into the vase with the handle of a watercolor brush or a pencil.

FIGURE 65. Finished vase for a flower or weed arrangement. On the top a White Waxy glaze was used. The remainder of the piece was stained with Barnard Clay slip on the bis-cuit; then most of the slip was sponged off, leaving the texture heavily stained. The vase was fired to cone 10 in a reduction atmosphere.

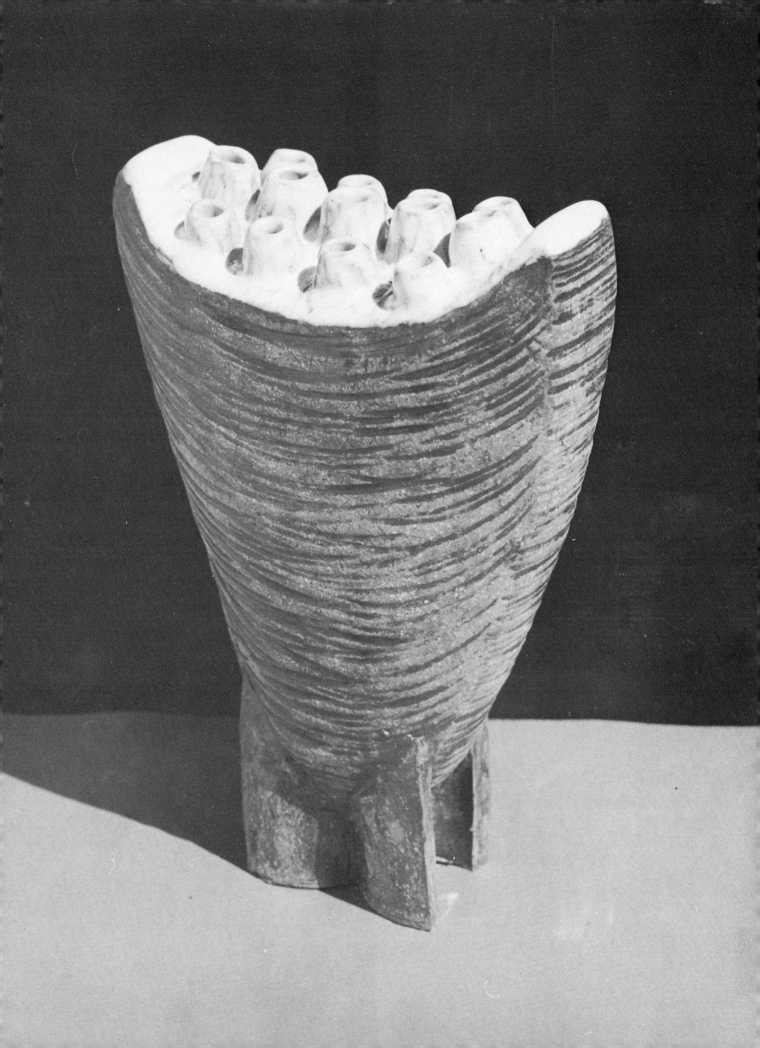

FIGURE 66. A variation of the basic technique of wrapping clay around a paper mold. Seven paper tubes were spaced on one long sheet of clay and a second long sheet of clay was laid over the tubes. The spaces between the tubes were pinched together. When the flower holder was set upright, a gentle spiral shape was given to the form for stability.

5. WRAPPING CLAY AROUND A PAPER TUBE MOLD

To utilize this simple method of forming you must begin by becoming a "collector." You might start by saving the cardboard tube, or core, from a roll of paper kitchen towels, or by salvaging old mailing tubes. You can obtain large tubes from a store that sells rugs. Carpets and rugs come wrapped around heavy cardboard tubes that are usually thrown away.

Start your project by selecting the size tube needed for your purpose. (See Figures 67 through 71.) Then find a piece of cloth with a coarse texture, such as burlap, monk's cloth or knitted material, and spread it out on a table. Roll out a slab of clay on top of the cloth. The cloth will give the clay an interesting texture that you can use to good advantage.

With a needle, cut out two rectangles of clay, about three-eighths inch thick and three and a half times as wide as the diameter of the paper tube. Lay the paper tube on one rectangle, and place the other rectangle on top of the tube. Lift the bottom edges of the *bottom clay slab* to meet the edges of the *top clay slab* so that the seams divide the circumference of the tube.

Pinch the edges together firmly enough so they will *stick* together. Lift the paper-tube-and-clay form and set it upright. You may want to pinch the edges together again, just to insure firmness. Since these edges are part of the forming process, they are also an authentic part of the form itself. They can be decorative but should not dominate. Pinch the edges once more after trimming to give them a final finish.

In preparation for making the bottom and top, trim the edges of the clay tube. Then turn over the clay tube (with the paper tube still inside) to a position that allows for adding the bottom. First, however, bevel the edges of the bottom of the clay tube. Then from a scrap of clay cut out a circle to the size of the bottom hole or slightly larger.

Now pinch the inside edge of the circle so the sides of the circle are beveled. Brush thick clay slip on the beveled edge and put the circle in place to form the bottom. If you need to, take a wooden stick and paddle the bottom plug, or circle, solidly into place.

Weld the seams thoroughly and smooth off the bottom. Set the clay tube right-side-up and pull out the paper tube. If the tube is left inside, the clay will crack as it shrinks upon drying. When the tubular vase is dry, it can be bisque fired.

There are many intriguing variations of this technique. Three seams, instead of two, on a medium-size tube could be interesting. A large tube might have four seams. After a large clay tube is formed, the seams can be pinched to change the shape from a cylinder to a more complex form.

FIGURE 67. After a paper tube has been selected for the purpose, clay is rolled out on a piece of burlap. Two rectangular pieces of clay, three and a half times as wide as the diameter of the tube, are cut out.

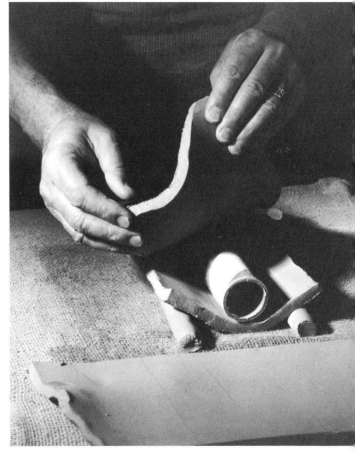

FIGURE 68. The paper tube is placed on top of one rectangle, then the edges of the rectangle are raised with coils of clay. The second rectangular piece is placed over the paper tube.

FIGURE 69. The edges of the clay rectangles are pinched together.

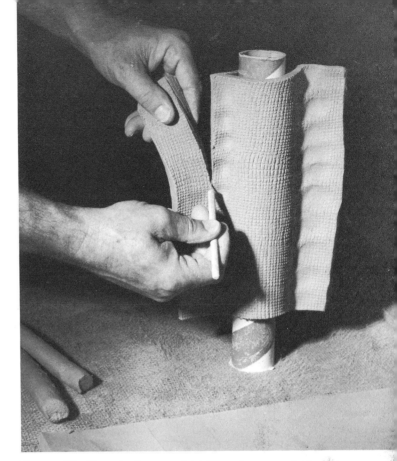

FIGURE 70. The tube is set upright. The edges are pinched together again, more firmly this time, and the excess clay is trimmed away.

FIGURE 71. A round piece of clay is cut to plug the bottom of the tube. The inside edges of the circle are beveled, and the plug is welded into place with clay slip.

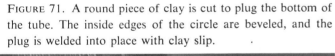

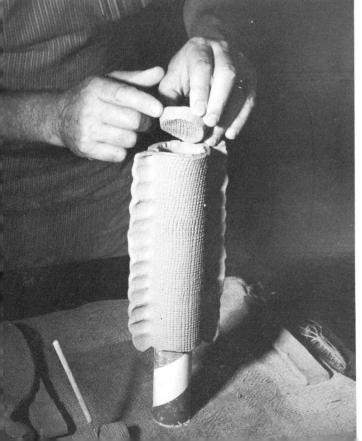

FIGURE 72. Finished vases. The bisque clay was stained with Barnard Clay slip to bring out the texture. The inside, the top edge and the pinched edges were glazed with Waxy Turquoise glaze. The firing was to cone 10 in a reduction atmosphere.

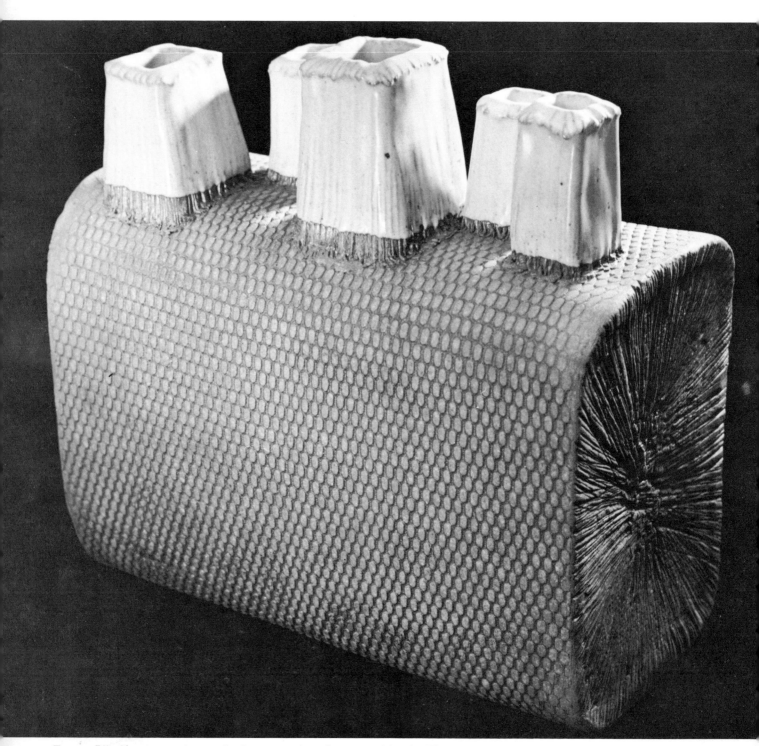

FIGURE 73. Clay wrapped around a form to make a five-spouted bottle. The texture is an imprint of a knitted nylon laundry bag. The clay was stained with Barnard Clay slip, and the five spouts were glazed with White Waxy glaze to cone 10 in a reduction atmosphere.

6. WRAPPING CLAY AROUND A FORM

While cylindrical shapes can be made easily on a potter's wheel, most oval and rectangular forms are more successfully produced by means of slab construction.

Look around for some shapes to use as the core, or form, for your clay object. Square or rectangular bottles are useful, as are the many rectangular food containers, cans and boxes to be found in the kitchen. You can use a wooden box, a block of wood or a brick. Use your ingenuity in making a selection. In the illustrations showing this construction method (Figures 74 through 80), a cardboard container for dry tempera paint was chosen as the core, or form, for the clay shape.

When you have chosen your form, wrap it neatly in several thicknesses of newspaper. Fasten the paper with glue tape, scotch or masking tape. If the clay is quite wet, the newspaper will absorb some of the moisture. Don't be concerned if the clay sticks to the paper. The core will slide out of the newspaper wrapping, and the paper can easily be pulled off the clay.

With a rolling pin, roll out a good-size lump of clay in several directions, making sure the rolling pin is dry. You can use strips of wood as guides for thickness if you wish. The clay works best if it is three-eighths inch thick. Making the clay form will be difficult if it is only one-quarter inch thick.

To obtain one type of texture, roll the clay onto a piece of fabric with a coarse texture, such as burlap sacking, or try a piece of monk's cloth, hand-weaving, knitted material or an ordinary dish cloth. They all work well. In the illustrations the cloth is knitted nylon. It gives a beautiful texture somewhat like snakeskin.

After the clay is rolled, cut one *side* and one *end* straight. Place the newspaper-wrapped form on the clay so that the end of the form is one-quarter inch inside the straight side. Wrap the clay and the cloth around the form. Do not pinch the clay, but cut it where the edges meet.

With a modeling tool smear the two edges together. Take a coil of clay the size of your little finger and model it over the joint where the two edges meet. Pat or rub the joint with the nylon cloth to restore the texture. Pull the cloth off the form, and stand the form on its flat end. Now, using a needle, cut the surplus clay off the upright end. If the clay is very soft, let it dry for a while (heat will speed the drying). When the clay is stiff, the form can be removed. Shake or pull the form out. Remove any newspaper that may have stuck to the inside of the clay.

Bevel the inside edges of one open end of the clay form by cutting the clay with a needle. Cut a bottom to fit the hole from some clay scraps. Moisten the edges and fit the plug into the bottom. Work over the seams, patting the clay with a wooden stick.

Turn the form over and repeat the process. Cut the plug for this side so that it fits well. Smear soft, gooey clay on all edges and put the plug in place. This should trap air inside the form, which will hold the clay in shape. Pat the edge with a wooden stick. Now you may texture the ends. In Figure 78 the ends are textured with the edge of a square stick. Dry the form until it is firm. As the shape dries, set it in different positions to determine the best way to finish it. Do you want a foot for it to rest on? If so, do you want it on its side or on an end? Do you want a neck, a spout or a handle? While the clay is drying you can make some of the shapes needed to complete the pot.

In the accompanying illustrations the two small, squarish spouts were made by pinching small lumps of clay into hollow square shapes. The sides and edges were textured again with the edge of a square stick.

Put the spouts in place on the pot and scratch around them to mark their positions, then remove them. Scratch inside the markings and moisten these areas. Put soft clay on the bottom edges of the spouts. Now put the spouts in place and carefully weld them to the pot. When they are securely attached and all the finishing is done, cut the holes into the pot. Do this carefully with a wire-end modeling tool and weld the inside joints with a lead pencil. Now the two-spouted pot is finished. Let it dry slowly before the bisque firing.

FIGURE 74. The rectangular form is wrapped in several thicknesses of newspaper.

FIGURE 75. Clay is rolled out on a knitted nylon laundry bag to give it texture.

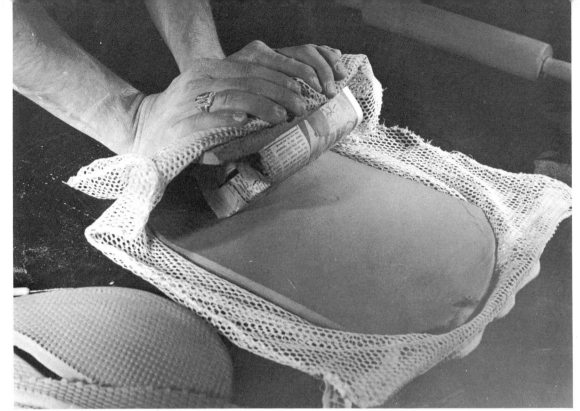

FIGURE 76. The clay slab and knitted nylon laundry bag are loosely wrapped around the newspaper-covered mold.

FIGURE 77. After the joint is sealed and retextured, the hollow clay form is prepared for plugs to seal both ends.

FIGURE 78. The ends of the form are closed with clay plugs and patted with a stick to weld them into place and texture the surface.

FIGURE 79. Tapered rectangular spouts are pinched out of lumps of clay and welded to the form. When the clay is firm, holes will be cut through them into the form.

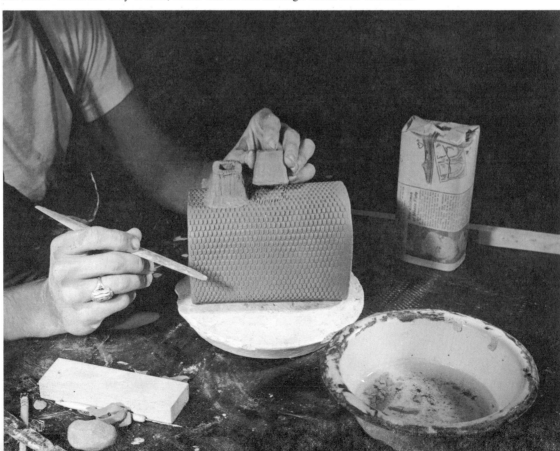

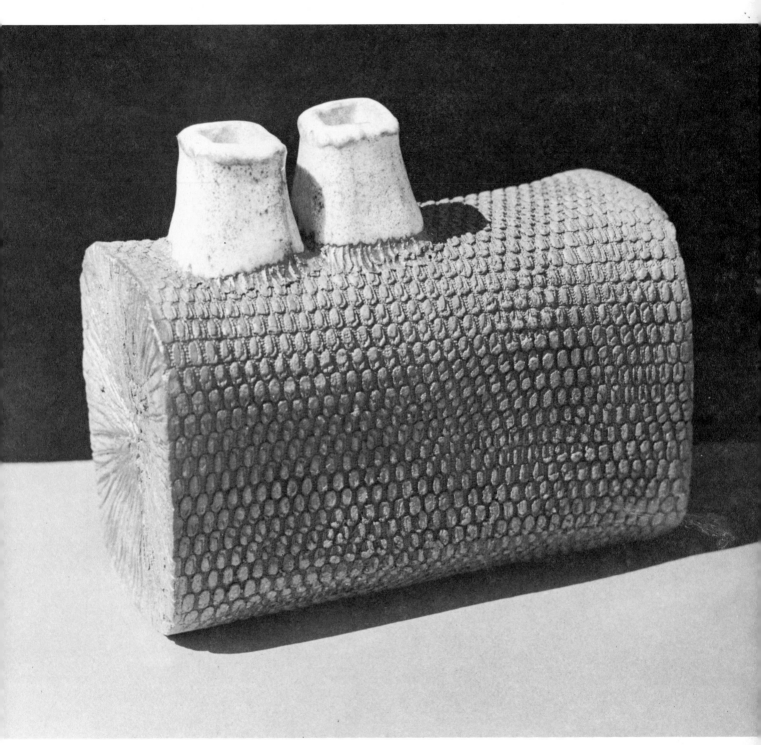

FIGURE 80. The finished bottle-shaped vase. Barnard Clay slip was used to stain the textured clay and White Waxy Mat glaze was applied to the spouts. The piece was then fired to cone 10 in a reduction atmosphere.

7. DRAPING CLAY OVER A CARDBOARD DRUM MOLD

The construction of a piece of pottery by using slabs of clay is an excellent forming technique. Slabs may be thin, medium-thick (about three-eighths inch) or thick (one inch or more). A medium thickness is generally preferable and most often used.

The slab can be formed by patting a lump of clay with the hands until it becomes a wide, thin sheet; by rolling out the clay on a cloth with a rolling pin; or by slicing a large lump of clay into thin sheets, using a cord or piece of twisted wire as a cutting tool.

The slab of clay can be twisted, stretched, cut, assembled or joined into innumerable forms. By various methods it can be treated as cloth, metal or wood. But the methods of construction that are typically those of clay are best. Any method mentioned above for preparing the clay is good. But in the project illustrated (Figures 82 through 90) it was *rolled out* to the desired size and thickness. To prepare it in this manner you will need a dish towel, a rolling pin and a breadboard.

The best kind of clay for making slab constructions is that mixed with grog (a pre-fired clay crushed until it looks like sand). Grog can be purchased in varying grain sizes. The percentage of grog used with clay is from fifteen to twenty per cent, although some potters use as much as thirty per cent. Grog can be kneaded into a fine-grain pottery clay. A grog mixture has a number of advantages. Grog will keep clay slabs from warping; it will eliminate some shrinkage; it permits the use of thicker pieces of clay without running the risk of cracking or having work blow up in the bisque firing.

Start your slab construction by putting a good-size lump of clay on a breadboard covered with a dry dish towel. Roll the lump of clay into the desired thickness with a rolling pin, spreading it in many directions until the slab is one-half inch thick and larger than you need.

Since we are going to use *pre-textured* clay in this project, you must first think of a texture to enhance the surface of your clay slabs. Here is one simple way to create a handsome texture: First buy a thin sheet of Styrofoam from a hobby shop. (Better still, buy two or more sheets if you wish to experiment, or in case you make a mistake.)

In Figure 82, freely curving lines of varying lengths were pressed into the Styrofoam with a dull lead pencil. Short lines at right angles scattered over the Styrofoam were made by gently tapping the material with the edge of a mayonnaise jar lid. To proofread your pattern hold the Styrofoam close to an electric light. This will make the pattern easier to see. The lines, depressions or gouges making up the design in the Styrofoam should be close enough to create an overall pattern. The pattern should not be too scattered and thus appear "spotty." Restrain yourself when it comes to combining a number of shapes on one piece of the material. Keep the pattern *all circles, all lines* or *all squares*. It is extremely difficult to combine many shapes to produce a good, simple, overall pattern.

When the Styrofoam pattern is complete, lay it on top of your clay slab. Put another breadboard or a piece of cardboard over the Styrofoam. Now slide one hand under the bottom breadboard and put the other hand on the top board. Flip the whole thing over so that the clay slab is on *top* of the sheet of Styrofoam. Now with the rolling pin, *roll your clay just hard enough* to press it firmly into the Styrofoam. If you wish, lift a corner of the clay to see if the texture is being imprinted deeply enough. If you are satisfied, slowly and gently lift the clay slab, peeling it off the Styrofoam one corner at a time. The clay slab should be beautifully textured. Now repeat the foregoing process, as this project requires two identical slabs.

Next you must find a form over which you can drape your clay to give it shape. It is easier to shape it over a form or container that is curved. It is also less difficult to handle. A small tub, garbage can or cardboard drum all have possibilities. The tapering shape of a waste basket is excellent.

A cardboard drum twelve inches in diameter was used to form the slab constructions illustrated here.

Put a board on top of the textured slab of clay and flip it over. Now you can drape it around a curved shape with the texture facing outward. Let the clay slab dry until it is able to hold its shape. You can use an electric fan or a hair dryer to speed up the drying process.

To make a pot similar to the one illustrated you will need, besides two slabs constructed as described above, a slab of clay for the bottom. Roll clay onto a dry dish towel placed on top of a breadboard. Put several sheets of newspaper on top of the clay slab. Put another board on top of the newspaper and flip the whole thing over.

Now the clay is on top of the newspaper. As the clay dries and shrinks it can slide on the newspaper, which will keep it from sticking and perhaps cracking.

Roll out two coils of clay at least one inch in diameter and long enough to form the ends of the pot. Sponge the coils with water to keep them soft.

To assemble the various parts, take one of the curved, textured slabs of clay from the mold when it is *just firm enough* not to bend out of shape. Handle it gently so you won't mar the texture or bend it out of shape. Place one edge of it on the bottom slab of clay, then repeat with the second curved stick. Move the sides into place in the center of the bottom slab so that the ends are one-half inch apart. With a bowl of water and a long-handled brush used for oil painting, brush water around the bottom edge of the pot and up the inside edges of each slab where the ends will be joined.

If you wish, slip can be painted on the inside edges of the side slabs. Sponge water or slip on the large coils and place a coil inside, at one end of the pot. Now take a stick about one inch thick, two inches wide and approximately twelve to fourteen inches long and gently paddle the coil from the inside until it is wedged into place to join the two sides and to close this end of the pot.

Reach inside with one hand, while bracing the clay on the outside with the other, and pinch the coil to make a good joint. Brush the surfaces with water or clay slip. With a wooden modeling tool smear the clay coil and the ends of the slabs together. Smooth the surface with your fingers and pat it with the wooden stick, inside and out. Repeat the process with the other end.

Now weld the bottom seams together. Brush the seams with water again, unless the clay is still wet. Take the end of a long-handled brush and make a

FIGURE 82. A thin sheet of Styrofoam is scratched with a pencil to produce the incised design.

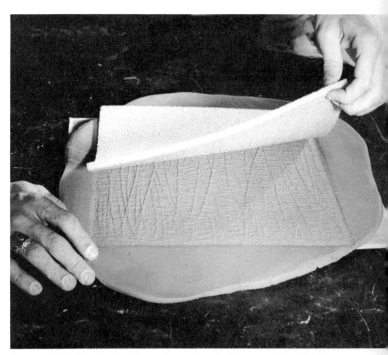

FIGURE 83. The incised Styrofoam is rolled onto a clay slab to give it texture.

FIGURE 84. Detail of textured clay slab.

FIGURE 85. The textured clay is draped over a cardboard drum and allowed to become firm.

FIGURE 86. Two curved, textured slabs of clay are placed in position on a bottom slab of clay.

FIGURE 87. A two-inch coil of clay is paddled into place to join the slabs and make a corner of the pot.

FIGURE 88. The outside of the coil and the ends of the slabs are carefully welded together.

FIGURE 89. A wooden stick is used to texture the ends of the pot. A lip rim has been made of clay cut from the base.

groove at the joints on the outside. Roll out a coil of clay the size of a lead pencil, lay it into the groove and weld and smooth this coil with your fingers — in order to fill the groove. Try not to damage the surface of the walls on the outside.

To make a perfect seam, weld the joints where the sides and bottom meet on *the inside of the pot,* smearing the clay from sides and bottom into one another until well integrated. Make a groove in the clay at the joint. With a coil about the size of a lead pencil, fill the groove and weld the coil in place smoothing the joint with your fingers.

With a needle, trim the clay slab on the outside of the base of the pot. Don't handle it. An inch or an inch and a quarter out from the base make another cut with the needle, parallel to the first cut and following the shape of the base. This provides you with a curved slab of clay that can be applied as a lip rim to the top edge of the vase. Repeat this on the other side.

Wet the top rim of the piece with water or slip, or both, and fasten the straps of clay in place. Weld the joints carefully from the *inside* of the container. With a square wooden stick, beat these slabs so they are pressed *downward,* or vertically. This should improve the joint, and at the same time — if a slight tilt is given to the tool — a beautiful texture will develop on the rim of the pot. That finishes all the work except what has to be done on the bottom.

The bottom can be finished in several ways. A slab can be added to make a continuous foot, smaller than the pot, but repeating its shape. This type of foot can be made, then areas of it cut off in order to make legs. In the pot illustrated no legs or lumps of clay were added, but the bottom edge was beveled inward. The bevel was then paddled with the edge of the stick to repeat the texture on the top of the pot. A repeat pattern or a repeat with variation of line, form or texture can create an interesting effect.

73

FIGURE 90. The finished pot has been glazed on the inside and on the lip rim with Blue-green Waxy glaze. The outside was stained with Barnard Clay slip, then fired to cone 10 in a reduction atmosphere.

FIGURE 91. Another variation of the same technique to produce a three-sided vase. The Styrofoam texture of circles on the clay was made by pressing glass jar tops into a sheet of Styrofoam.

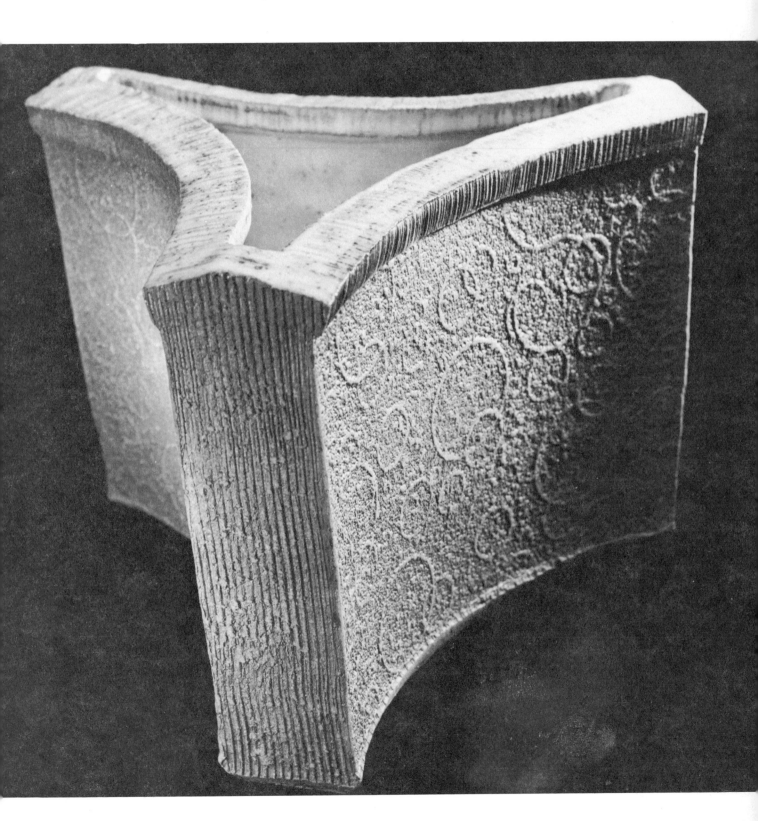

FIGURE 92. A vase made over a plastic bag filled with sand. The mouth and handles were glazed with Chun Chrome Green glaze, fired to cone 10 in a reduction atmosphere.

8. WRAPPING CLAY AROUND A PLASTIC BAG FILLED WITH SAND

For this project you will need a plastic bag filled with some sort of material to give it volume and weight. Sand is good; it is easy to procure and to use. It is heavy, however, and makes the bag bottom-heavy. Sawdust or peat moss would also work well as a filler. Pumice sand or gravel that is sold in markets for barbecue grills is lightweight and excellent for this purpose. The pumice sand can be used in the plastic bag in which it is packaged.

The bag should be half or two-thirds full so that its neck can be tied securely, even wrapped with string, so that it creates a cylindrical neck on the large form. Now the mold is ready to use. (See Figures 93 through 101.)

Roll out a large sheet of clay about three-eighths inch thick onto a piece of cloth. Place the bag on one half of the clay slab. Fold the other half of the slab over the top of the filled plastic bag. Now gently coax, pat and stretch the clay over the bag so that its edges will come together. Pinch the edges together firmly. Pat and mold the clay around the lower part of the tied-up neck of the bag. Cut away excess clay. Do not try to make a very long neck of clay; if you wish a long neck, it can be added later.

The bag can now be placed upright. The form will change a little bit, so pat the clay firmly around the bag and pinch the seams together in order to make the clay fit the bag-mold rather snugly.

Tie a long piece of cord to the neck of the bag, and hang the bag with the clay around it to some overhead support so that it hangs freely.

Now, if you wish, gently paddle the seams flat with a wooden stick. Take wads of clay and fill up any holes or irregularities. Paddle the clay some more to give it its final form. Let the bag hang free until the clay is firm enough to hold its own shape.

Cut the bag down and open it. Pour the contents out, then pull the plastic bag out through the neck. Wrap a moist cloth around the neck and leave it there until the clay in the neck becomes moist and pliable.

Turn the clay form upside-down in a vase, jar, bowl or other form that will support it without damaging the neck. Now the base can be considered. A short coil foot can be made, legs can be applied, a tall slab cylinder can be formed for a foot, or an irregular foot can be formed from coils of clay. Perhaps coils of clay will fit this form best.

After you have softened the bottom with clay slip

and welded a base coil solidly to the pot, build the foot to the size and height you think most appropriate. For one kind of texture, scratch the foot vertically with a dull lead pencil. Now texture the bottom half of the pot. The edge of a piece of tree bark or a broken stick makes an excellent texture tool with which to pat the damp clay form. Let the foot dry long enough so it will hold the weight of the pot when it is set right-side-up.

When you turn the pot over you can decide how to finish the top. It can have a short, small or wide neck. It can have one or more long necks or spouts if you think they are suitable and useful. Handles may also be applied. Because it was wrapped in damp cloth, the clay of the neck should be moist and pliable. Cut the edges evenly and wet them with slip.

You can add coils, slabs or pre-formed cylinders to finish the neck or necks. When the form is completed, the surface can be textured in any way you desire. Paddle it as you did the base, or scrape or polish it to give it as much interest as you wish while keeping the finish subtle and beautiful. The pot should be set aside to dry slowly so it can be bisque fired.

FIGURE 93. Fill a plastic bag two thirds full of sand, sawdust or (as in this illustration) "Vermiculite." Roll out a sheet of clay and place the filled plastic bag on it.

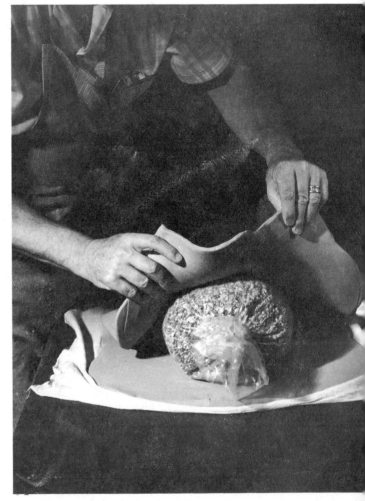

FIGURE 94. Fold the clay over the bag, stretching it until the bag is covered.

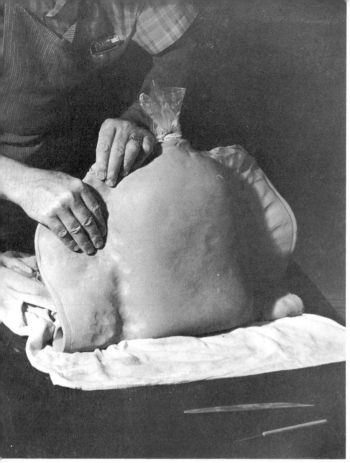

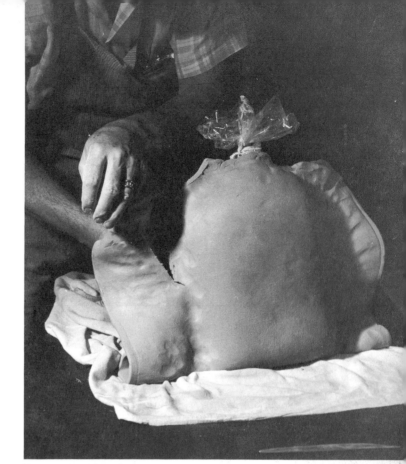

FIGURE 95. Place the bag upright and pinch the edges of the clay together.

FIGURE 96. Cut the surplus clay away and again pinch the edges of the form firmly together.

FIGURE 97. Smooth the edges or seams so that the bag is covered evenly with clay.

FIGURE 98. Tie a cord around the neck of the bag and hang it up to dry until the clay becomes firm. Then paddle the bag lightly to give it its final shape.

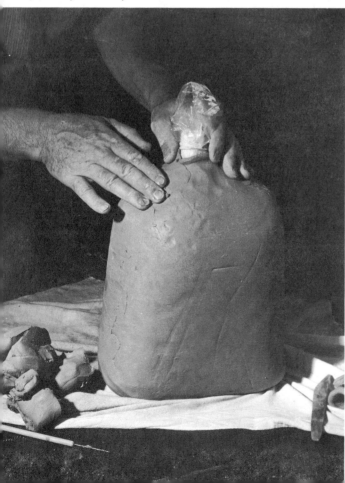

FIGURE 99. Texturing the clay. Here it was paddled with the broken end of a stick. The base was added, using coils of clay. The neck had been formed previously and is ready to add to the pot.

FIGURE 100. The plastic bag is opened, emptied and then pulled out of the clay form.

FIGURE 101. The finished vase is stained with Barnard Clay slip, glazed inside with Turquoise Waxy glaze and fired to cone 10 in a reduction atmosphere.

80

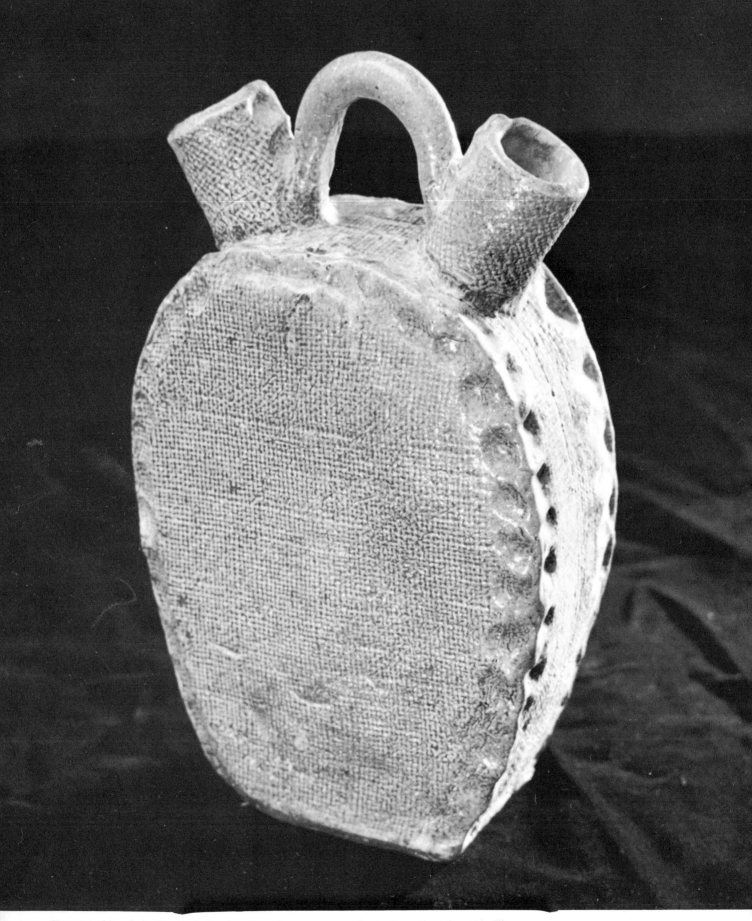

FIGURE 102. A bottle made by forming clay over a pre-formed cardboard mold. The pinch marks were purposely left. The bottle has been salt glazed.

9. DRAPING CLAY OVER A PRE-FORMED CARDBOARD MOLD

There are times when a potter will wish to build a closed form out of clay. He can't drape or mold clay over a solid form, since there is no way of removing the form once the clay is dry. There are several methods for making closed forms, but most of them are involved, time-consuming and call for some experience, and the chances of success are questionable. The best solution for the beginning potter is to make a cardboard core construction (Figures 103 through 110).

To do this you must begin by making a mold out of cardboard. Corrugated cardboard boxes are the best source for your raw material. Draw the shapes you want directly on pieces of the cardboard, or first cut your shapes out of paper and then trace them on the cardboard. Then with a mat knife, a razor blade or a metal-cutting tin snips, cut out the cardboard shapes.

Arrange the cardboard pieces in the way you wish to make the mold, and tape the edges firmly together. Use *glue tape,* not scotch tape or masking tape. Put the tape on the outside of the edges to hold the pieces together. Leave the bottom of the cardboard form open, and the core mold is ready to use.

On a piece of cloth, roll clay into two or three large sheets about three-eighths inch thick. Lay your core mold on its side on a sheet of clay and trace around it; then cut out the clay piece with a needle. Repeat this on another sheet of clay for the opposite side. Lay one cut slab of clay on top of the cardboard form, while the form is resting on the other piece. Now you have two sides of clay in place.

Measure the other two sides and cut them out of clay slabs. Wrap these around the vertical sides of the cardboard form so that it is completely enclosed except for the bottom.

Because the clay is wet and plastic, it will be easy to push the edges together to make perfect joints. The surface can be textured at this time.

The clay-covered cardboard form can now be set upright. If desired, a neck or other detail — except the base — can be added to the pot. Before this is done, the pot should be allowed to dry for a while. Allow plenty of time, for the clay will shrink as it dries. When it is quite firm it will reach the maximum point of shrinkage, at which time the clay — especially at corners or seams — will start to crack. It is at this point also that the clay will become firm enough to hold its own shape unsupported, and the cardboard mold can be removed.

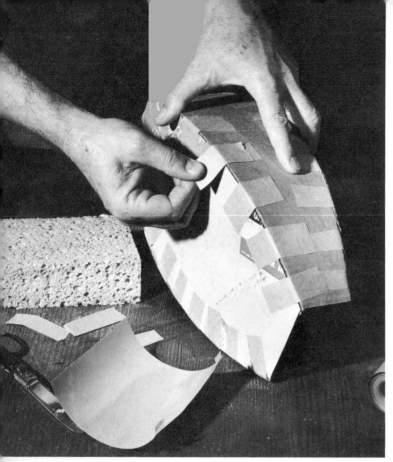

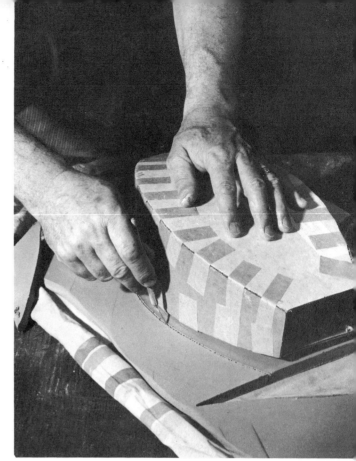

FIGURE 103. Corrugated cardboard pieces are assembled and taped together to form a core or mold.

FIGURE 104. The cardboard core is used as a pattern from which slabs of clay are cut.

FIGURE 105. The cut slabs of clay are placed to cover the cardboard form. The edges of the wet clay slabs are pinched and modeled together.

FIGURE 106. While the clay is still quite wet, a rectangular tube of clay is attached to one end of the form to make a neck for the vase.

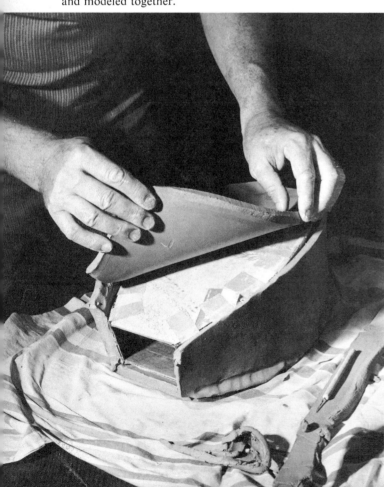

FIGURE 107. When the clay is quite firm (nearly ready to crack) the moist cardboard form is rolled up and pulled out of the open bottom of the vase.

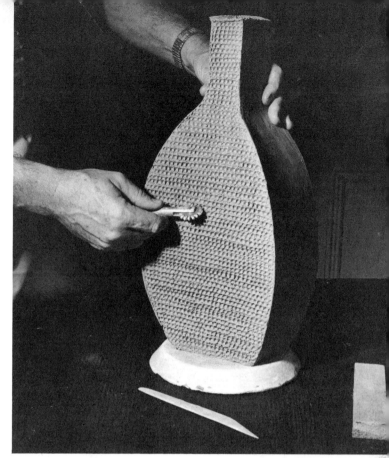

FIGURE 108. A small aluminum texturing wheel is used to decorate two sides of the vase.

Contact with the wet clay makes the cardboard quite damp and softens the glue on the paper tape. So now it is a simple matter to reach inside the form through the open bottom and pull out the cardboard. The cardboard may have to be folded and crumpled inside the clay form in order to remove it.

If you feel it is necessary to weld the seams of the pot from the inside, it will be easy to do so at this point. Now the pot is nearly complete. All it needs is a bottom and, if you wish, a foot.

Set the pot upright on a slab of clay; the bottom edges of the pot will make an impression in the wet clay. Cut out this shape to make a plug for the bottom. Now stand the pot upright in a pan filled with a half inch of water. Let the bottom edges soak until they are quite moist. Then remove the pot, lay it on its side and weld the bottom plug in place. If you wish, you can add a foot rim to complete the pot. After the pot has been put aside to dry thoroughly, it is ready for the bisque fire.

FIGURE 109. A slab of clay is inserted into the open bottom of the vase to complete it; then a foot was added.

FIGURE 110. The smooth side, the top and the inside of the vase were glazed with MG 2 Turquoise glaze. The texture was stained with Barnard Clay slip, and the piece fired to cone 10 in a reduction atmosphere.

FIGURE 111. A variation of the same construction method. Red clay was rolled onto a piece of burlap for texture. White Tizzy glaze was poured over part of the form; then the piece was fired to cone 7 in an oxidation atmosphere.

FIGURE 112. A cardboard core was used to form this planter, which was glazed with Turquoise Waxy glaze containing magnetite to form specks.

FIGURE 113. Clay was draped over a pre-formed cardboard mold. It was textured with a rolled-up strip of corrugated cardboard, stained with Barnard Clay slip, and glazed with G Mat 3 Mottled Blue.

FIGURE 114. This garden vase was made with the same construction techniques. Plywood was used as a mold instead of cardboard; the form was pulled out the top. The enclosed top, made of slabs, was added after the mold was withdrawn. The vase is four feet high and weighs one hundred pounds.

FIGURE 115. Seven hump-molded bowls assembled to make an attractive serving tray.

10. DRAPING CLAY OVER A HUMP MOLD

Pots made by the hump mold method can be both functional and beautiful. When imagination is given full play, this technique offers endless variations.

There are many ways to make hump molds. Large boulders or pebbles worn smooth by a river or the ocean can be gathered and used as hump molds. Moist sand can be mounded up and patted into shape, covered with cloth and used as a form upon which to drape clay. A solid lump of clay can be shaped, allowed to become firm and then, covered with a piece of cloth, used as a mold. Clay can also be shaped and covered with plaster of paris to make a waste mold — by removing the clay and filling the cavity with plaster. When the mold is knocked off, a fine plaster hump mold remains (see p.94). All of these techniques are excellent.

Styrofoam was used to make the hump mold illustrated here (Figures 116 through 122). This versatile material is inexpensive and readily available at hobby shops. It is extremely lightweight and easy to cut.

Purchase a thick piece of Styrofoam. To draw the symmetrical silhouette of the form you want, fold a sheet of paper over twice and cut out the shape so that all sides are even. Unfold the cut-out center piece of paper, place it on the piece of Styrofoam and draw around the pattern. An asymmetric form can be sketched freely on the Styrofoam and cut out with a coping saw. (It may be roughed out first with a straight saw.) It may also be cut out with a paring knife or roughed out rapidly with a wood rasp, then refined and smoothed with a piece of coarse sandpaper.

It is important to carve the bottom side of the mold — the flat side — in such a way that it makes a convenient hand-hold which can be used to pull the clay shape away from the mold. With a paring knife you can cut and dig out two holes — one large enough for the fingers to fit in, the other hole for the thumb, with a handle in between the two holes. Now the mold is ready to use.

Lay a breadboard or drawing board on a table, and cover it with a dish towel. Place a piece of clay — not too wet and sticky, and preferably with grog in it — on the dry cloth and beat it into a thick pancake.

With a clean, dry rolling pin, roll the clay in various directions until it is three-eighths or one-half inch thick. (If the clay is only one-quarter inch thick it is quite difficult to handle.)

Put the Styrofoam hump mold right-side-up on the

FIGURE 116. The hump mold is carved from a piece of Styrofoam with a wood rasp.

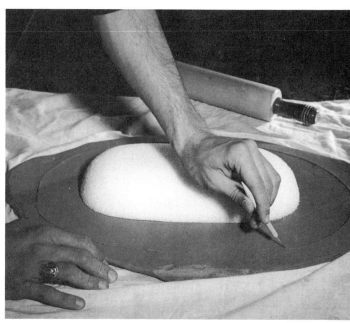

FIGURE 117. A slab of clay is cut into an oval shape, much larger than the mold.

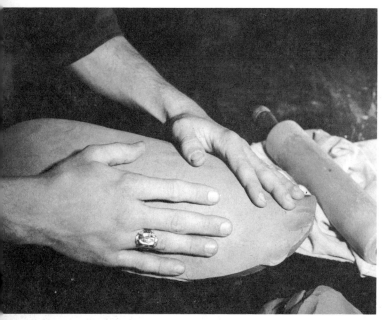

FIGURE 118. The mold is propped up on a brick; the clay slab is draped over the hump and stretched and pressed to fit it.

FIGURE 119. The outside surface of the clay form is textured with the broken end of a brick.

clay and draw around it, leaving a wide margin to allow enough clay for covering the mold. Cut away the extra clay with a needle. Next, place the mold upside-down on the center of the slab of clay. Slide one hand under the clay and cloth, place the other on the mold, and flip everything over. Set the mold and its clay covering down on a brick or block of wood to raise it up from the table. Peel the cloth off the clay. Now gently coax the sheet of clay to fit the hump mold snugly. Press it, compress the edges, stretch the bottom a bit, pat it gently. Cut any excess clay away from the bottom edge. A cheese cutter is an excellent tool for cutting away surplus clay; a needle will also work well. Keep patting the clay into shape, trimming away excess clay.

Now you are ready to apply texture. The most satisfactory hump-molded pots are those with an interesting surface texture. The broken end of a brick or kiln shelf support is an excellent texture tool; even a broken kiln shelf will work. Tap the clay gently and evenly all over with your texture tool. It is a good idea to turn the clay mold right-side-up to inspect the edges. If they are too thin, patch and texture them, and then cut them even with the bottom of the mold.

Turn the clay mold upside-down again, and add a bottom to it. You can put a coil foot on it, or three or four lumps for feet, or other clay devices to make a bottom, or stand, for the pot. When applying lumps for feet, it is best to mold them onto the pot by building them up a little piece at a time. If you make clay marbles and try to stick them onto the pot for legs or feet, there's a good chance that at least one of them will come off in the bisque firing.

To level the foot, place a board on top of it and

FIGURE 120. Small wads of clay are modeled onto the base of the form to make feet.

FIGURE 121. When the clay is firm enough to hold its shape, the hump mold is removed.

FIGURE 122. The finished hump-mold bowl. It is stained with Barnard Clay slip on the outside, glazed on the inside with Pale Blue Waxy Mat glaze, and fired to cone 10 in a reduction atmosphere.

stand back to see that it is parallel with the tabletop. Now that the clay is firm, it is possible to alter the shape somewhat. You can cut the sides one-half inch down all around, or curve them in places. If this is done well it gives character to the form.

Here is one precaution: *The clay cannot be allowed to dry on the form.* Clay shrinks as it dries; because the mold doesn't shrink, the clay will crack. When the clay is dry enough to hold its shape, turn it over and pull the mold out of the clay form. Now any imperfections on the inside can be patched. The edges can be made true and smooth, even polished with a wooden tool. Allow the pot to dry upside-down if the top is level. The shaping process is now complete, and the pot is ready for bisque firing.

Plaster Hump Molds

Plaster is probably the best material for making a hump mold suitable for the forming of pots. It is, however, difficult to use. It can become quite messy and bits of plaster scattered around the studio may get mixed into the clay. When this happens, the plaster will blow out a piece of the pot in firing and perhaps ruin it. But the plaster mold is the most durable of all and can be used for many years. For that reason alone it may be worth the extra time its construction requires.

To make a plaster mold, first model a form out of a solid piece of wet clay. (See Figures 123 through 129.) Pound and paddle it to a rough shape. If the clay is allowed to get partially dry or stiff, the form can be refined by scraping the surface. Be sure the form has

FIGURE 123. Clay has been molded into a hump. Plaster is applied to the hump to make a waste mold.

FIGURE 124. Plaster is spread over the clay form to a thickness of at least one-half inch. The top is leveled off to make a flat bottom on the mold.

FIGURE 125. When the plaster is set, the clay is pulled out of the waste mold.

FIGURE 126. The waste mold is lined with soft soap, then plaster is poured into it. Before the plaster has completely set, a handle is cut into the hump.

FIGURE 127. The waste mold is knocked free of the plaster hump mold.

no undercuts. The clay must stick to a non-porous surface such as a varnished board, a sheet of glass, a slab of marble, or linoleum.

Now mix a batch of plaster and stir it thoroughly until it is fairly thick. Take a handful of the plaster and carefully spread a thin coat to cover the clay. Let the remaining plaster get buttery in consistency. Then put a *thick* layer of plaster over the *thin* layer, so that it will be at least one-half inch thick. Let the mold stand for a half-hour or more from the time the plaster is mixed.

FIGURE 128. The waste mold and the hump mold separated. If the waste mold is intact, it can be used for making another mold or for forming clay.

FIGURE 129. The surface of the hump mold is scraped smooth.

FIGURE 130. This long, narrow bowl was formed by draping clay over a hard, moist, solid hump of clay. Blue-green Waxy glaze was used on the inside. The outside was textured with a piece of insulation brick which had been scratched with a knife.

When the plaster becomes quite warm, it is *set*, or as hard as it ever will be. You can then remove the clay and plaster from whatever surface it rests on. Carefully dig the clay out from the plaster waste mold. When all the clay has been removed, put a thick layer of soft soap over the inside of the plaster mold. Remove the excess soap and let the surface dry a bit. Mix another batch of plaster and fill the mold. Let the plaster stand until it is buttery, then carve a hand-hold on the bottom inside surface.

When the plaster is fully set and warm to the touch, it can be tapped free from the plaster waste mold. A wooden mallet hammered against the rim of the mold will work the two pieces apart.

If the waste mold remains in one piece it can also be used for forming clay. The hump of plaster — the hump mold — can now be scraped smooth and, after drying for a day or two, it is ready for use.

The method for using this mold is the same as that previously described.

FIGURE 131. A bowl formed by draping clay over a granite boulder. Brown G Mat 3 glaze was used on the inside. Barnard Clay slip stains the outside surface. It was fired to cone 10 in a reduction atmosphere.

FIGURE 132. A triangular form made from a plaster hump mold. It was textured on the outside with the end of a broken brick, and glazed with Pale Blue and Blue-green Waxy glaze.

FIGURE 133. An illustration showing how four hump-mold forms have been joined to make an unusual serving tray.

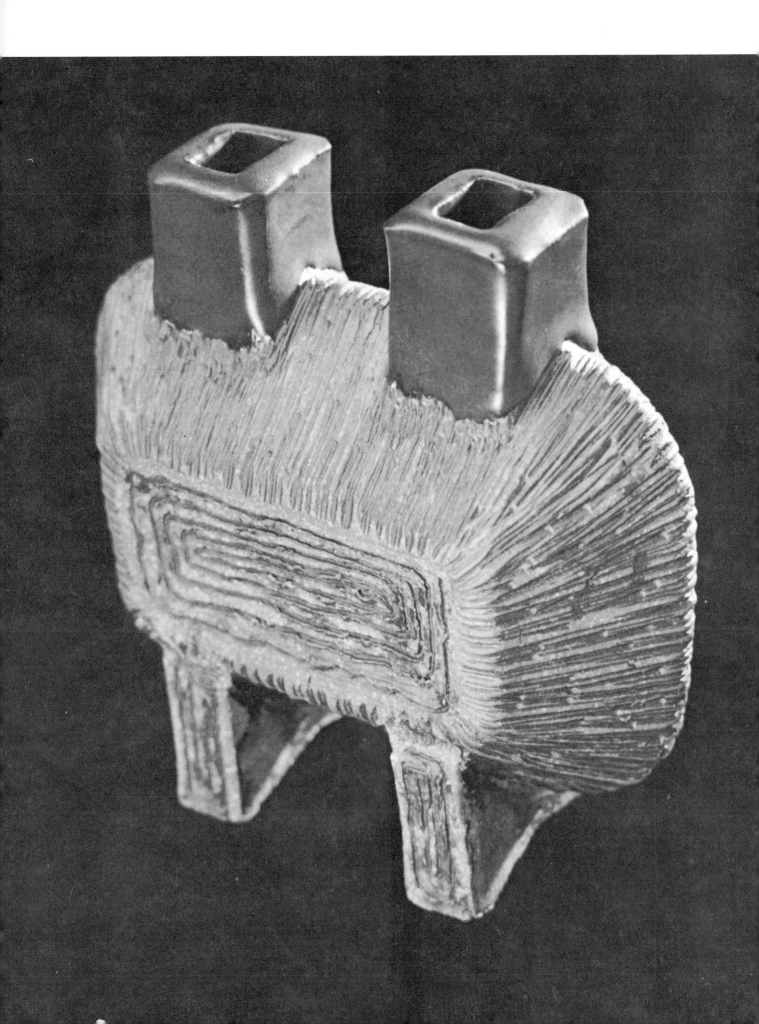

FIGURE 134. Two paper plates from a market fruit stand were used as molds. The clay was draped inside the plates and the halves were joined. Texture was applied with a square stick.

11. DRAPING CLAY INTO A "FOUND" MOLD

Look around the kitchen or in a hardware or department store for a form you can use as a "found" mold. There are many. Square or rectangular cake pans, or any pans with straight sides, are good. Those with slightly tapering sides are even better. Inexpensive tin or aluminum pans will do nicely. You may also find interestingly shaped plastic containers that will function satisfactorily as molds. The latter are often appealing and encourage quick-forming techniques for making clay forms.

Don't make any extensive plans for producing ceramic gifts in volume for your friends! This technique takes time and care, and not infrequently the piece is destroyed in the final fire. Square or rectangular forms of this variety are most difficult to make well. They may warp and crack in many places. If two out of three emerge from the kiln in good condition, you can consider yourself quite an expert.

The forming process is as follows (Figures 135 through 146): After selecting a container for your mold, make a lining for it out of heavy wrapping paper, being sure that it fits the pan well. Make sure also that the paper liner is large enough to be folded over the edge of the pan and taped in place on the outside with masking or cellophane tape. With this done, your mold is ready. The paper liner keeps the clay from sticking to the pan; it will peel off easily.

On a dish towel placed over a drawing board, roll a lump of clay into a large sheet about three-eighths inch thick. Set your pan mold right-side-up in the middle of the clay slab, and trace around the bottom of it onto the clay surface. Now lay a side of the pan on the clay, adjoining the bottom, and mark the clay again. Mark off all the sides of the pan onto the clay in this way. You are making a pattern on the sheet of clay, just as you made the paper pattern for the lining. The clay pattern, however, works better if it is slightly *smaller* than the paper pattern, thus allowing for the thickness of the clay.

Cut out the clay pattern. Place the paper-lined pan mold upside-down on the clay pattern. Slide your hand under the dish towel on which the clay rests. Put your other hand on the bottom of the pan and flip the whole thing over. The clay will sag into the mold. Coax it into sagging even more. Lift the edges of the clay slab and gently press it down to fit the mold. The bottom edges of the clay pan will not be sharp, but this is not necessary.

The seams at the corners must be thoroughly welded together, using the following procedure: With the eraser end of a pencil press the clay firmly into the corners of the pan, making gouge marks in the corners. Fill these gouges with clay. Then make a ball of clay and press it into the bottom corners of the clay pan. You may have to add more clay in order to fill them. Smooth the clay surface. When the clay pan is finished, trim the edge off even with the edge of the pan. Set the pan mold aside until the clay is slightly firm.

Next, lay a dish towel over a drawing board and roll out another sheet of clay larger than the pan mold and three-eighths inch thick. Then place the pan with the clay pan in it upside-down in the center of the second sheet of clay, and remove the pan mold. Then remove the paper. Weld the seams thoroughly where the two clay forms join by making grooves and filling them with clay coils. Now, a half inch or an inch out from the rim of the clay pan, cut the second sheet of clay to make a flat rim for the pan. This will improve the appearance of the clay form and it counteracts warping.

When the clay is firm, and while the form is still upside-down, you can add feet to the container if you wish. There are several ways to make them. They can be made with either coils or slabs, although the latter are probably better. Roll out another sheet of clay and with a needle cut clay straps in right-angle shapes. Before the feet are added, wet and score the bottom of the clay pan where they are to go. Then put thick clay slip on these spots; add the feet and weld them solidly onto the clay form.

When you have finished, you can turn the whole form right-side-up to dry a while longer. Put a board on the bottom of the clay form. Put one hand on this board and the other under the bottom board and flip everything over. Remove the top board. With a needle, cut out the inside of the top clay slab to complete the rim. Weld the inside seams together solidly. Put a piece of newspaper over the top of the clay pan, then put a board on top of that and *flip the whole thing upside-down again.* Let it dry for a while.

When the piece is quite firm, some sort of texture may be added. In Figure 145 texture is combed into the clay with a short length of saw from a child's carpentry set. Be sure to dry the completed pot very slowly and thoroughly before it is bisque fired.

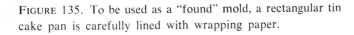

FIGURE 135. To be used as a "found" mold, a rectangular tin cake pan is carefully lined with wrapping paper.

FIGURE 136. A sheet of clay is measured and cut to fit inside the paper-lined pan.

FIGURE 137. The slab of clay is carefully pressed into the paper-lined pan.

FIGURE 138. After the corners are welded together, the top is trimmed.

103

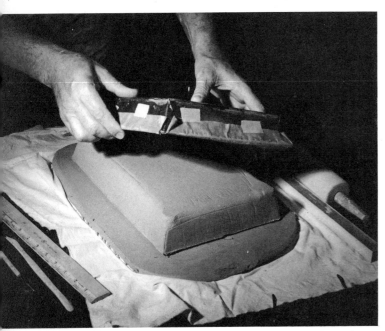

FIGURE 139. The firm clay pan is turned over onto a large sheet of clay, and the tin pan is removed.

FIGURE 140. The edge of the large clay slab is trimmed to make a rim for the clay pan.

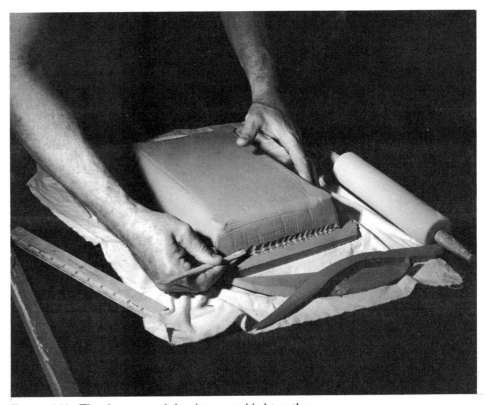

FIGURE 141. The clay pan and the rim are welded together.

FIGURE 142. The welding grooves are filled with coils of clay.

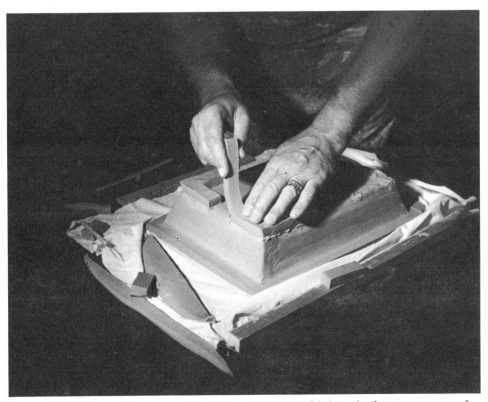

FIGURE 143. Slabs of clay are cut in right angles and welded to the bottom corners of the pan to make the feet.

FIGURE 144. The pan is turned over and the center of the slab forming the rim is removed.

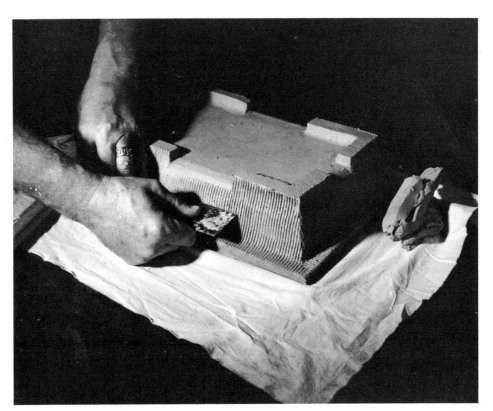

FIGURE 145. The outside of the clay pan is textured with a saw blade from a child's toy carpentry set.

FIGURE 146. The finished planter (or platter) is glazed with Blue and Green-blue Waxy glaze inside and fired to cone 10 in a reduction atmosphere.

FIGURE 147. Slabs of clay were attached to make a foot for this sling-molded pot, which was then carved while the clay was leather hard. White Oatmeal Waxy glaze was used on the bowl, which was fired to cone 10 in a reduction atmosphere.

12. DRAPING CLAY INTO A SLING MOLD

This is a simple technique for forming clay pieces that often intrigues beginners. Although it is limited in scope, it is excellent for one-of-a-kind shallow containers. This method of construction is also good for making a free-form piece. Free-forms should be kept quite reserved, however, for if the shape is too "busy" it will not be successful.

The method is as follows (Figures 148 through 152): Select a piece of cloth that will stretch a bit in several directions. A piece of knitted fabric or a double thickness of cheesecloth will work well. (Because they do not stretch, old pieces of sheeting or burlap are not as good.) Cut the piece of fabric twice as large as the clay form you wish to make.

Turn a stool or small table upside-down. Tie a piece of cord to each corner of your cloth; tie the other end of each cord to a leg of the stool or table. Now you have a sling mold.

Roll out a piece of clay three-eighths inch thick. Cut it into a long, narrow oval. Put this oval slab of clay into the cloth sling. Now take the edge of a jar top or a curved potter's rib and gradually press down the center of the oval. Keep stroking the clay, gradually molding it into a shape at least one inch in depth.

Note: This is the point where most beginners fail. By its own weight the clay naturally takes a shallow form. If it is not pressed into a deep enough shape, both the form and the workmanship are bound to be poor. Don't be too easily satisfied. Work to press the clay into a shape that could contain a fair quantity of liquid. The clay and the cloth will stretch slowly into shape. The cloth will support the clay and maintain the shape.

Let the clay dry until it can hold its own shape; then remove it from the sling. It is advisable to work, carve or model the edges of the pot to make them clean, even and interesting. They may be sharp and square or round or beveled, inside and outside. The outside surface may be scratched, scraped or gouged to produce a texture if you wish. The clay should be kept at the softest point possible, yet still hard enough to retain its shape.

Now you are ready to think of a plan for adding a base, or feet. The design of the feet (or foot) will probably determine the excellence of the final form. The base may be scraped flat to make a very simple foot, or an oval coil of clay might be attached to the bottom to raise the form slightly. Round or square lumps of clay could be added from which legs for a more complex and imaginative base could be designed.

After you've decided on the base you want, turn the bowl upside-down. To support the bowl in this upside-down position take a soft lump of clay and pat it into a mound *the shape of the inside of your pot, only smaller.* Cover this clay support with a paper towel and place the bowl on it. If you are adding a coil or lumps, mark the areas where they are to be attached to the base and score those areas. Wet the scored areas with clay slip, then score them again and wet them a second time. Attach the feet solidly, for they have a habit of coming off easily either in drying or in firing. While your bowl is still upside-down, place a board across the feet to make certain the bowl is level. Then let the pot dry until it is ready for firing.

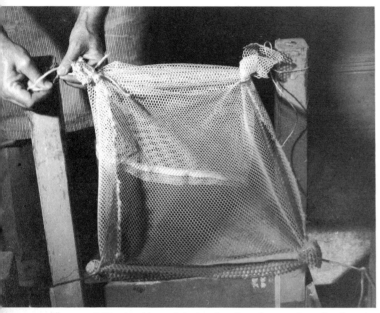

FIGURE 148. A piece of knitted nylon from a laundry bag is made into a sling mold by tying the corners to the legs of a table.

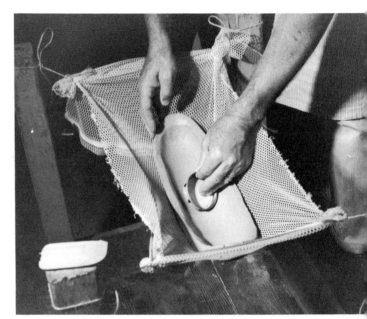

FIGURE 149. An oval slab of clay is laid on the sling and pressed into a long form with a jar lid.

FIGURE 150. After the clay form has become firm, it is turned over onto a long, good-size lump of clay which supports the container; then feet are added to the bottom.

FIGURE 151. When the clay form is dry enough to hold its shape, the top edge is trimmed and finished.

FIGURE 152. The sling-molded pot was glazed on the inside with Chun Celadon glaze and fired to cone 10 in a reduction atmosphere.

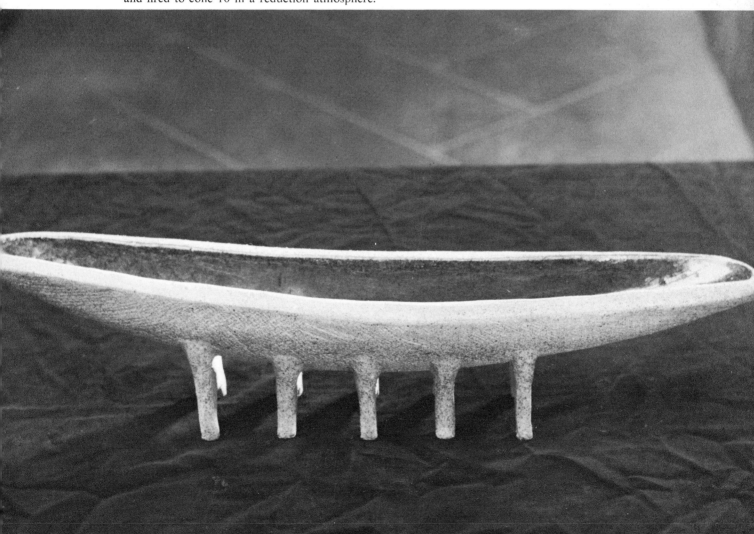

FIGURE 153. Small pinch pots with variations in texture form this wind bell. It is strung together with rawhide boot lacings. Metal fins to catch the wind are made from thin sheets of copper.

13. MAKING A PINCH POT

Pinch pots afford an excellent opportunity to create textured effects on clay, if the textures selected are indigenous to the pots' handmade characteristics. Texture should be treated not as an end in itself, but with the somewhat crude and primitive qualities of the hand-formed pinch pot in mind. If this is done, some unusual and interesting tactile surfaces can be achieved.

Making a pinch pot is one of the simplest ways in which to become acquainted with the texture of clay itself. It is also one of the easiest ways of forming and a wonderful exercise for the hands.

Natural, red or buff clay should be used for pinch pots and all other pots. The white clay or talc body blended for low temperature work is not suitable for beginning or advanced work because it is too difficult to manipulate successfully. Red or buff clays are a delight to work with, for they respond especially well to this technique.

To make a pinch pot, the shapeless mass of prepared and slightly damp clay is divided into lumps the size of a clenched fist. The clay lumps should not be *too* damp and just large enough to cover with both hands. (See Figures 154 through 162.)

Take a lump of clay and pat it over and over again

— in the way you would make a snowball. When the ball is round and smooth, hold it in one hand and pinch it with the other, pressing the thumb into the center so that you make a small dent in the clay. Revolve the ball of clay and pinch again. Revolve and pinch, revolve and pinch until you gradually make a hole in the clay ball. Don't pinch too hard. Don't rush. Keep the form round and make a thick bowl. As you pinch, keep the walls and the edge even until the walls are about one-half inch thick.

If the clay cracks, smooth the cracks over with your fingernail or the flat side of a paring knife. The heat of the hands can gradually dry the clay too much. If this happens, moisten your hands with water. But use only a little of it — too much water will spoil your work.

After one bowl is formed, put it aside and make a second bowl as nearly resembling the first as possible. Now wet the rims of the bowls with a little water and weld or model the edges of the two bowls together with the end of a modeling tool, a paper knife, a lollipop stick or a tongue depressor. Smear some of the clay from the edge of the first bowl onto the edge of the second. You are sealing up the air trapped in the form you are making.

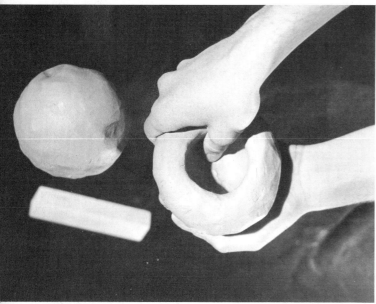

FIGURE 154. Take a ball of clay and by pinching it repeatedly with one hand as you revolve it with the other, make a hole in it.

FIGURE 155. Keep pinching and revolving the ball of clay to make a bowl. Make two bowls in this manner.

Make a coil of clay as big around as your little finger. Put this coil of clay over the joint to fill the space you made with the wooden tool. Smooth out the coil of clay with your finger and fill up any little holes with extra scraps of clay.

If the shape you have made is too irregular or flat because not enough air is trapped inside, you can blow it up. To do this, as previously described, make a marble from a piece of clay; push and model the marble onto the end of your clay shape. Using a pencil, punch a hole through the center of the wart and through the wall of the clay form.

Now place your mouth over the hole and blow gently into the clay shape until it puffs up. If you blow too hard, you will blow a hole into the clay. If this happens, patch the hole with your modeling tool and some clay. Blow up the form again and push the hole together with your teeth and lips. Trap all the air you can in the clay form. Press the hole together, fill it up, and cut away the "wart" of clay. The air pressure now inside the bowl will hold the clay in shape, just as air in an automobile tire keeps it from going flat.

Find a piece of wood one inch thick, two or three inches wide and six to eight inches long. This is a very useful tool. Use the stick to gently slap or paddle the clay shape until it is smooth. Then you are ready to texture the surface. In Figure 158 a meat tenderizer mallet was used to texture the clay. You could also use the end and edge of your flat stick paddle as a texture tool, or you could wrap string around the stick and paddle the clay with that. Experiment with textures on scraps of clay before selecting one for your vase. If, in this method of forming, the tool leaves its marks, this will provide the most authentic textural treatment of all.

When the shape is textured, set it aside to get *firm*, but *not hard*. Let it stand overnight if you wish. To rush the drying you can put it in the sun for one-half hour, turning it often, or you can place the piece over a radiator heater or put it in front of an electric fan, turning it frequently. An electric infra-red heat lamp or a hair dryer also works well in helping to dry the clay rapidly.

While the clay is drying think how you wish to finish the shape. Do you want to stand the shape on its end, or on its side? What kind of base or foot do you wish

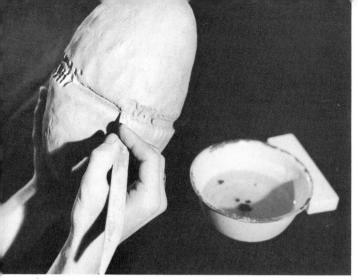

FIGURE 156. Put the edges of the bowls together and weld the seams.

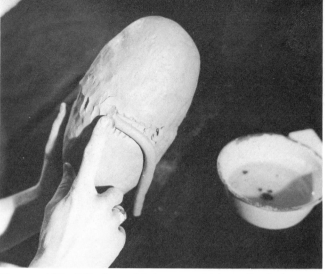

FIGURE 157. Fill the welded seam with a coil of clay and scrape the surface smooth. Air trapped in the container holds the clay in shape.

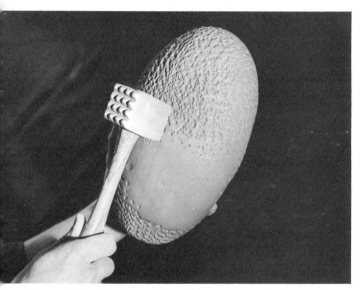

FIGURE 158. Pat the surface with a meat tenderizer mallet to produce one kind of texture.

FIGURE 159. Pinch a bowl-shape out of a small ball of clay to form a base, or foot, for the pot. Patting the surface with the edge of a wooden stick provides texture.

FIGURE 161. Solid wads of clay welded to the top of the form will create spouts for the vase. When the clay is firm, a water-color brush handle or a pencil may be used to punch holes through the center of each lump of clay.

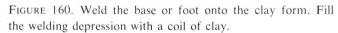

FIGURE 160. Weld the base or foot onto the clay form. Fill the welding depression with a coil of clay.

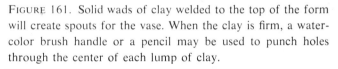

FIGURE 162. Texture on the finished vase was emphasized by staining the bisque clay with Barnard Clay slip. The top was dipped into Waxy White glaze. It was fired to cone 10 in a reduction atmosphere.

to use? You can make a base while the shape is drying.

To do this take a small ball of clay and pinch it, just as you did the first pinch pot, to form a base. Texture the base if you wish. The base shown in the illustrations was textured by paddling it with the edge of the stick paddle. While the base is drying, you can shape a neck or spouts.

When the form and base are both firm, put soft clay and water on the parts you are going to weld together.

Add the base to the form, using your wooden modeling tool to smear the two together. Make a small coil of clay to fill up the depressions created by the modeling tool. Make a good joint also on the inside of the base. Let the shape dry a little longer, until it can stand on its base without sagging.

Now you can attach the spouts or neck. Attach them in the same manner that the base was attached. If you want small spouts, they can be made from solid lumps

116

FIGURE 163. A small, simple pinch bowl. Texture was applied with the end of a lollipop stick and lines were incised with a pencil. The glaze is Waxy Oatmeal.

FIGURE 164. This triangular pinch pot was textured by paddling the surface with a wooden stick grooved with a saw blade. The glaze is Turquoise Waxy.

of clay, then added to and modeled on the form. Holes can be punched into the spouts by pushing the point of a lead pencil through them, thereby opening holes into the main form.

If a neck is to be attached to the form instead of spouts, it is important to attach it first, *then* cut holes through it that open into the form. A wire-end modeling tool is excellent to carve out this hole.

Now the pot is ready for bisque firing.

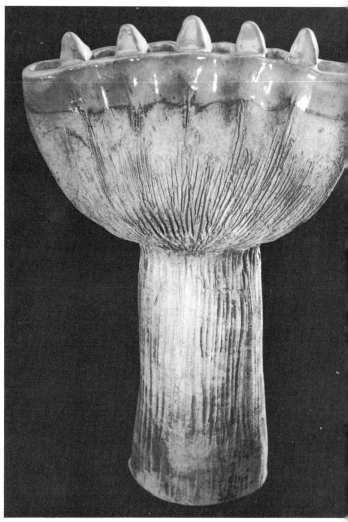

FIGURE 165. This pot was pinched into an angular form. The design was applied with the tip of a pocket knife blade. A base was pinched out for this bowl. The glaze is Pale Blue Waxy.

FIGURE 166. This is a simple pinch bowl. After forming, it was flattened, then pinched clay marbles were inserted to join the sides between the holes. The base is a pinch pot added to the bowl. Texture was scratched into the clay. The glaze is Chun Mottled Blue.

FIGURE 167. This is a variation of the form illustrated in the step-by-step demonstration. The texture is applied by combing the clay surface with a metal comb used for grooming dogs. The eleven-spouted top was glazed with Blue-green Waxy glaze. The clay was stained with Barnard Clay slip and fired to cone 10 in a reduction atmosphere.

118

FIGURE 168. The basic idea for this coil-built form was an imaginary seed pod. It is glazed on the inside with Albany Clay slip. The depressions on the outside are filled with Albany slip, which is not satisfactory because it is too shiny.

14. COIL BUILDING

Only a few potters have explored the full potential of coil-built pottery, yet this technique offers unlimited possibilities for form and decoration. It is a very practical method of construction and an exciting one. Most beginning potters go to great lengths learning the *techniques* of coil building; however most of their efforts produce rather uninspired, run-of-the-mill shapes.

Great emphasis is placed on smoothing out the coils and perfecting the circular form to imitate wheel-thrown pots. While it is true that beautiful Indian pottery was built with coils which were finished by being rounded and smoothed, the Indian potter was concerned chiefly with *function*. We, on the other hand, can afford to direct our major efforts toward a unique self-expression in creating textures and decorative qualities. When we have a potter's wheel for throwing round pots by hand, and industry to produce well designed functional pieces, it seems pointless to copy them in a laborious hand-modeling technique. Yet in order to relieve the monotony of mass-produced pottery and functional objects, we need the fruits of honest creative power to produce work that is individual and unique.

If you have ever tried to work with clay coils you are aware that no matter how you may coax and beat them, coils seem determined to take every form other than a circle. Instead of forcing them into shapes that seem unnatural, why not let the coils themselves dictate the form?

Before you grab a wad of clay and start rolling coils, however, stop for a moment. Let your imagination roam freely. What are you going to make? Coils can be easily guided into beautiful organic shapes. Think of Bryce Canyon and its fantastic forms, the rock formations of Monument Valley and the Grand Canyon, the eroded terrain of the "Bad Lands." These unusual shapes and textures are only a few of the many that can act as sparks to ignite your creative powers.

It is not necessary to have a fixed idea of the finished piece before you start developing the shape. Let the nature of the clay guide you as you build. Do not force or abuse it. Acquire a little of the potter's discipline and respect your hands and tools.

Clay for coil building should have as little shrinkage as possible. It does not have to be as plastic as pottery clay, especially the type of clay used for throwing, but it should be quite open or coarse-grained. You can convert a regular throwing clay into a good coil-building clay by wedging grog into it. Wedge the clay thoroughly in order to distribute the grog evenly, then break off a lump of clay and pat it into a pancake about one-half inch thick. This makes the base. Pinch or cut it into a simple shape, but not a round one. An oval is excellent, or you might wish to try a cloverleaf or a five-lobed form. Put this clay shape on a plaster bat or board. (See Figures 169 through 176.)

Now roll a coil of clay. To make a good coil you will need to experiment because it isn't as easy as it looks. If the clay is rolled out on top of the table, only the fingers should be used, not the palms of the hands. As you roll the coil back and forth, spread and close the fingers to control the clay.

The diameter of the coils is for you to decide. Small pots will naturally take thinner coils; large pots can be built from either thick or thin coils. If thin coils are used, however, it will take a longer time to build a large pot.

Remember that the weight of the pot will depend upon the size of the coils with which you start. If weight isn't too important, larger coils can be used. But it *is* important that constructing a coiled pot not become tedious because the result will show your boredom and weariness. A skilled potter can generally build a three-foot coil flower holder in about six hours.

Now that you know how to make a coil of clay, roll a fairly thick one for the first layer. Moisten the base of the pot slightly and place the coil around the perimeter. Do not use much water during the construction.

With your thumb, smear the coil into the base on the inside. On the outside, push the clay coil onto the base, using your fingernail and spacing the fingernail marks irregularly.

It is imperative that the methods of construction be evident in the finished pot. This principle helps to produce a good piece of work. It is tempting to fake the fingernail process by merely building up a nest of coils and pushing down dents or holes in them. This is a false technique and the result will look false.

Strive for interesting texture as you work. You must be careful, however, that the texture will not be the first thing that fascinates the observer. One must first be aware of the pot *as a whole* — as a vase, a bottle or a bowl. Texture should always be secondary in importance.

A fairly clear outline of the individual coils together with the irregularly spaced marks made by the fingernails will make a handsomely textured surface. Since the inside is carefully smoothed and the coils well blended together, the shapes of the coils on the outside surface do not have to be destroyed for the sake of function. To add variety to the coil texture, small segments of coil can be wrapped into spirals and applied to the wall of a pot, while other areas can be filled in with short pieces of coil, or flattened balls of clay can be interspersed with the coils.

Coil after coil can now be put into place, the inside blended smoothly and the outside thumbed interestingly with the fingernail. Do not make a long coil that wraps around and around the pot. Evenly spaced spiraling coils become monotonous and may produce the effect of a woven basket.

Work first on one side of the pot and then on the other as follows: Place one coil *completely around* the top edge of the pot and model it into place. Next, put a coil only *half-way around* and finish modeling it. Now put a coil on top of this one but only a quarter of the way around the pot and thumb it into place. Finally, turn the pot around and repeat this procedure on the other side. These coils of different lengths, thumbed into place, will give tremendous surface interest and charm, as opposed to the monotony of a continuous spiraling coil.

Design as you build. If a coil is placed slightly *outside* the one beneath it, the wall of the pot will begin to flare at this point. If a coil is built slightly *inside* the one underneath, the wall will begin to slope inward. In this way the shape is controlled. The shape should not be developed by stretching the wall of the clay after it is formed because it will *look* as though it had been stretched. Also, if you do this, you will start tiny cracks that invariably split during the firing.

The pot must not be constructed too rapidly. If the walls are built up hurriedly, the weight will become too great for the bottom coils, and the pot will begin to sag. If this happens you will find it is usually better to discard the pot rather than try to prop it up and attempt to repair it.

To build a coil pot correctly, work until the walls are just slightly unstable, then stop. In some cases (depend-

ing on the temperature and humidity in the room) the open air will stiffen the clay sufficiently to allow you to resume work in a short time. If you want to hasten the setting-up process, let an electric fan play on the pot or use an infra-red heating lamp. Setting the piece in the wind and the sun will also work. Be sure the shape is the way you want it before drying the pot at all. Once the clay stiffens it will no longer yield to your wishes.

If you are interrupted during the coil building, you

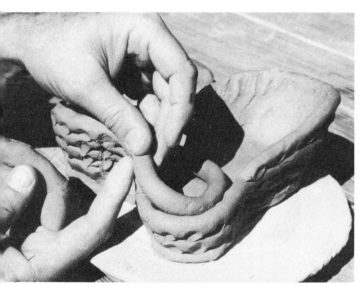

FIGURE 169. The third coil of a tri-lobed base is textured into place.

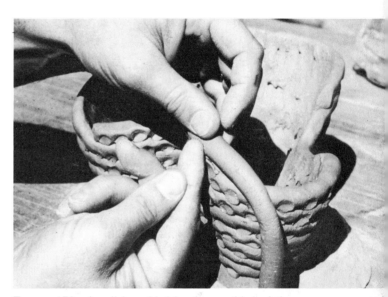

FIGURE 170. A coil is welded in place a third of the way up the wall.

FIGURE 171. One neck is being completed. Notice how the walls are closing in for the three necks to this vase.

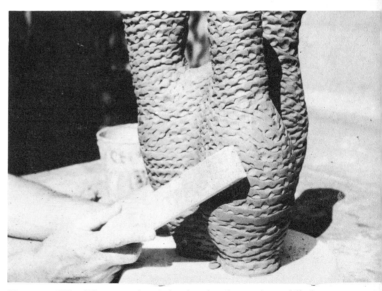

FIGURE 172. The completed leather-hard pot is paddled to unify the form.

FIGURE 173. This bisque-fired pot is stained with Barnard Clay slip.

FIGURE 174. The Barnard Clay slip is sponged off the surface, leaving only enough to stain the depressions. This enhances the texture.

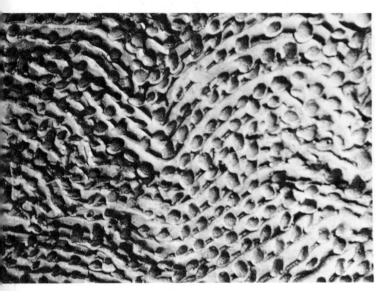

FIGURE 175. A close-up detail of texture achieved by the coil building method.

FIGURE 176. The completed pot. It is glazed only on the inside and lip with MG2 White Satin Mat glaze and fired to cone 10 in a reduction atmosphere.

can cover the pot with a plastic bag for an hour — or for a week or more. It will remain in good condition for additional work.

The top of the pot must be plastic enough to add the additional coils of clay required to complete it. So, before starting to dry out the pot, you might cover the top lip with a damp cloth, aluminum foil or a narrow strip of plastic.

It is possible to use slip to weld the coils together. But the slip should not mar the outside appearance. In fact, it really shouldn't be necessary at all. A good potter sees to it that his clay stays at just the right consistency to be welded perfectly, yet not be so moist that the pot will lose its shape.

When the shape of the pot is completed, it should be allowed to set to a leather-hardness. At this point it is

FIGURE 177. This coil-built vase won a prize for sculpture in a national ceramics exhibition.

important to "pull the shape together" by patting the outside surface with a wooden paddle. The high spots can be slapped back into shape, the low spots minimized, and lumps can be taken out so that the form will become more unified. Too much paddling can destroy the surface or cause cracks, so do it gently.

The finished pot should be dried very slowly and then bisque fired.

FIGURE 178. A variation of the three-lobed, three-necked, coil-built vase. This vase is 24 inches high.

FIGURE 179. A seven-necked vase glazed on the inside only with MG2 White glaze. A glacial escarpment in Glacier National Park inspired this form.

FIGURE 180. Free-standing, slab construction vase assembled from pre-textured, pre-formed slabs. Clay was stained with Barnard Clay slip and fired to cone 10 in a reduction atmosphere. Glaze is Oatmeal Waxy.

15. ASSEMBLING FORMS AND FREE-STANDING SLAB CONSTRUCTION

It is only after making quite a number of pots and becoming familiar with a variety of construction methods that the more complex ones should be attempted. By this time you should already know several methods of shaping clay. You should be expert at welding edges or seams together so they will not crack in drying or firing and know exactly how wet or how dry your clay should be for bending, paddling, stretching or welding edges. You should also know how firm the clay must be to hold its own shape.

You should be fairly sensitive to form, proportion, balance and function — all the qualities that go into making a beautiful pot. By now you have been exposed to a number of techniques and should be ready to utilize your own ideas in combining several of them in a single clay piece. Before you start, however, it is a good idea to make several sketches in order to develop those ideas. They may be altered as you work, but at least you will have a general plan to serve as a starting point and model to check your progress.

You might try building a free-standing slab construc-tion. While this is not a project for a beginning potter, you should now be ready to try it.

To begin your clay construction, roll out several good-size slabs of clay on pieces of cloth. Apply different textures to each slab if you wish. Pre-form some of the clay slabs. You can do this in many different ways. You might try *draping* clay over drum shapes, paper tubes or over the edge of a box to make a good right-angle shape, or *wrapping* clay around boxes or oval shapes. Or you could make some forms by the pinching process or by the coil method, and then assemble them. Let the pre-formed clay objects dry until the clay will just hold its shape.

From this point on you are on your own to express your individual feelings about clay. Variation in design is endless. Try your wings and be free!

One point of departure would be to assemble similar forms with slight variations, or *unlike forms*, so as to create a unified multiple-form. The accompanying illustrations include suggestions for such composite construction methods.

129

FIGURE 181. These five rectangular pots were made by using the technique of wrapping clay around a form. The surface was paddled with a piece of broken brick. The pots were then assembled on a slab of leather-hard clay placed on a kiln shelf. The pots were staggered, then joined with moist clay coils. The clay is a red color, glazed inside with White Stony Mat, fired to cone 10 in a reduction atmosphere. Joining pots in this manner makes a functional flower holder for a narrow table or shelf.

FIGURE 182. Eleven bowls were made by the pinch process. A leather-hard slab of clay was placed on a kiln shelf, on top of which the pots were arranged. Coils of clay were used to connect the bowls. The completed form was fired for bisque and glaze on the slab of clay to prevent cracks from developing due to shrinkage strains. *Insides* of the bowls were glazed with Pale Blue Waxy glaze with ilmenite in it. The piece was fired to cone 10 in a reduction atmosphere.

FIGURE 183. Five pinch pots textured by paddling the surface with the end of a broken stick. The pots were joined while moist (the connecting pieces should be fairly thick and curved to withstand the strain of firing). The pots should be assembled on a leather-hard slab of clay on top of a piece of kiln shelf, then bisque fired and glaze fired on the slab to counteract difficulties in shrinkage. Waxy Oatmeal glaze was used on the inside. The piece was fired to cone 10 in a reduction atmosphere.

131

FIGURE 184. This vase was formed by wrapping clay around cardboard tubes, then texturing it with a meat tenderizing mallet. The forms were assembled by using coils of clay which were modeled into the forms. The inside was glazed with Turquoise G Mat 3; the outside was left unglazed.

FIGURE 185. Three vases built by the coil method and joined together. They stand three feet high. White MG2 glaze was used inside and Barnard Clay slip on the outside. The piece was fired to cone 10 in a reduction atmosphere.

16. PREPARING POTS FOR THE KILN

Digging your own clay from the back yard or from a creek bed is a romantic idea, but this method of obtaining raw material also has its drawbacks. It takes time to prepare properly, and clay for forming pots must be of a good quality; if it is not, it is likely to crack or warp in the drying or firing process. Unrefined clay may not take as high a temperature as you wish, or it may take more than you have available. So if you want the fun of digging for clay, be prepared to make some test pieces to see if the material meets your requirements.

You can buy clay already prepared in plastic bags from a hobby shop. Quite often a nearby pottery, brick or sewer-pipe factory will sell you clay that will be excellent for your work. The ceramic magazines in public libraries furnish names of sources where it can be obtained. Be sure to buy from a store that can supply all the pertinent information about the specific clay you intend to use.

The beginning potter eliminates problems if he buys clay already prepared. He will have quite enough to think about and overcome without additional worries in his first experience as a potter.

KINDS OF CLAY

There are pottery clays for making earthenware that will fire from 1800° F. to 2000° F. These are the most popular and widely used clays and offer the lowest practical range for firing. The intermediate temperatures range from 2000° F. to 2175° F. and produce either a soft stoneware clay or a hard earthenware. Hard stoneware or soft porcelain is fired from 2150° F. to 2300° F.

Choose clay with a firing range suitable to the available kiln. If earthenware clay is fired to too high a temperature, it may melt or splinter into many pieces when it cools. Stoneware clay fired to too low a temperature will be soft and porous. Pots made from it will chip easily and vases will leak.

COLOR OF CLAY

You can buy white or buff clay that becomes pink or yellowish when fired, or a dark red clay. All of these colors are available at various firing temperatures. The white clays are generally the least plastic; the buff clays are always plastic and the most versatile. Red clays are also extremely plastic but much harder to clean up in the work area and more limited in color range.

CLAY BODIES

Clay and clay-like materials are blended to be fired at given temperatures to produce certain colors. Each different blend is to be used in *one kind of forming process*. These blends are referred to as *clay bodies*. Natural clays such as China clay and ball clay can be purchased in dry form. The potter must measure the clays, mix them, and wait several days or weeks for the clay body to age. Then it must be wedged or kneaded before it can be used. (Ideally, after wedging the clays should be aged and then wedged again.) The mess, time and energy consumed are not worth the small savings. It is far better to purchase a clay body already prepared, de-aired and packaged in a plastic bag.

WEDGING CLAY

A prepared clay body is ready for immediate use without wedging. After several pieces have been made from it, there may be some remaining scraps. These should be kept in a separate plastic bag. They can be reconditioned by adding water to the bag and letting the clay soak for a few days. There may be left over some wet, sloppy scraps. These scraps should be put into another separate plastic bag, for the sloppy clay will be useful in small quantities to join parts. Clay can be dried to a good working condition by spreading it on a dry plaster bat until it is ready to be wedged. All plastic clay scraps that have been used should be wedged before the clay is used again to form a new piece.

To wedge clay, cut a lump in half with a wire, then slap the two pieces together again in a new position. You can slap them together in the palms of your hands, or down on a wedging table or board. Repeat this many times until the clay is of a very even consistency. Knead the clay on a table as you would knead bread. Be careful not to wedge air bubbles into it. Slap the clay on the table again and make one solid, smooth lump of it. Now it is ready to use. A thick slab of plaster of paris or a heavy wooden table top makes a good wedging board. A piece of canvas stretched over a table top will prevent the clay from adhering to it.

STORING UNFINISHED WORK

Wet clay cannot be added to dried-out clay successfully. If a pot is not finished in one work period, it must be kept moist until it is completed. To do this, cover the piece with a plastic bag or wrap it carefully in sheets of plastic. This will keep the pot moist for weeks. An old discarded icebox can be used for storing finished work, without a plastic covering.

DRYING POTTERY

It is advisable to dry finished ware slowly. Pieces dried too fast may crack or warp. When you think your pottery is dry, dry it some more, preferably with artificial heat. A heat lamp or an infra-ray red lamp is excellent for drying ware. Pottery can also be put into an oven heated well below the boiling point of water and kept there for several hours while it dries thoroughly.

CRACKS IN GREENWARE

If there are numerous or large cracks in your dried pottery, it generally takes less time to start all over again than to try to repair them. Repairing cracks is difficult and rarely successful. In attempting to moisten the dry ware, more cracks usually develop. Small cracks, however, can be mended in the following manner: Widen the crack with a pointed tool. Take some dry clay and moisten it with *vinegar instead of water*; wet the cracked area with vinegar as well. Force the patching clay into the crack and burnish the surface. As the patch dries, burnish it repeatedly. If you are lucky, you may be quite successful.

BISQUE FIRING

It is advisable to bisque fire all your pottery. Stack your very dry ware in the kiln. The pots may touch one another. You may set one pot inside the other, *but keep the pots at least three-quarters of an inch from the sides of the kiln.* Remember that clay ware is very fragile. Handle each pot with *both hands.*

Heat the kiln very slowly at the beginning, leaving the door ajar until all the steam has escaped. Turn the kiln on and off periodically, if necessary, in order to keep the temperature below the boiling point of water until the pots are really dry. Too fast a heat will turn the moisture in the clay to steam, which will blow its own way out of the pots and destroy them. Close the door and increase the heat *gradually.* Pots can also blow up at a temperature around 500° F. to 600° F. Continue to increase the temperature slowly between 900° F. to 1100° F., for it is between these temperatures that the bottoms of pots are likely to crack if the heat rises too rapidly. Most clay can be bisque fired as low as 1750° F. If the bisque fire is too high, the pots are *too difficult to glaze.* If it is too low, the pots are *too fragile to glaze.*

KILNS

Firing pottery does require a kiln. In any large city there are commercial enterprises that do custom firing as a business. A hobby shop will help to locate someone who will fire your ware. An adult evening class instructor or a college ceramics teacher can help you.

You can buy an electric kiln that will plug into an ordinary electric outlet. To help pay your bills you can make and sell pottery or, for a fee, fire pottery for other people. A kiln won't cost as much as a good camera, a set of golf clubs, fishing tackle or even a large party.

Small electric kilns are very inexpensive to fire. Besides clay, they can also be used to fire enamel or copper and to make stained glass or slumped glass ware. Electric kilns up to 18 x 18 x 18 inches are very practical. If a larger capacity is desired, two small electric kilns are better than one large one. Or a small *gas* kiln of five-cubic-foot capacity is better than a large electric kiln. Gas kilns seldom have less than five cubic feet of firing space.

Low-temperature electric kilns that fire up to 2000° F. are less expensive than high-fire kilns. You can fire to low temperatures in a high-fire kiln (one that will fire up to 2300° F.) A high-fire kiln will probably cost one quarter again as much as a low-fire kiln, but it will last longer and it is much safer. If, for example, you forget to turn off a low-fire kiln and it over-fires, your kiln will be ruined. This is not likely to happen with a high-fire kiln. For a small price you can purchase an automatic shut-off for an electric kiln. An electric kiln, however, can be used only for oxidation firing. This is its chief limitation.

GLAZES

You can purchase glazes from ceramic supply houses, where samples of fired tile will help you make a selection. There is an unlimited selection of colors, textures and special effects in glazes from which to choose. Most of them are in the low-temperature range, but many supply houses also carry glazes for medium and high-temperature ranges.

Prepared glazes may be purchased in dry bulk form to which you add water. If you pay more, glazes can also be obtained in ready-to-use liquid form. It is more interesting and much less expensive to purchase large quantities of colorless-base glazes in dry form and add your own colorants and water. You will also learn more by doing it yourself. Eventually you will *want* to make your own glazes with a small investment of inexpensive materials. This is not difficult; in fact, it is comparable to cooking. The only special equipment you will need is a gram scale, or balance. Then simply follow instructions found in pottery books and ceramic magazines.

Pick out a simple recipe and purchase the materials required. Balance your gram scales. Now set the gram weights *for the amount required of the first ingredient in the recipe.* Weigh the material and dump it into a bowl. Check off this item. Weigh out the next material and dump it into the bowl with the first material. Continue until all the ingredients are weighed according to the recipe. Now add water slowly and stir the glaze until it is the consistency of thick house paint. Run the glaze through a fine (50 mesh) screen. It is best to screen the glaze twice, so it will be thoroughly blended. Put the glaze in a jar and label it carefully. It is now ready for use. The procedure is that simple.

In the beginning you should follow the recipes *exactly*. Later you may wish to combine several recipes or alter one. With enlarged understanding of your materials and added experience you can create your own glazes.

Looking at the myriad recipes for food, you wonder that still another might be concocted. Yet each new issue of the selfsame magazine offers new varieties and combinations of food. It is the same with glazes. There are always more to be discovered.

GLAZING

Glazes may be applied by brushing, dipping, pouring or spraying. *Brushing* glaze on a pot is done only when small quantities of glaze are available. It is a tedious and difficult method. It takes practice to do it well, but it is an excellent technique when expertly done. *Pouring* a glaze is easy and practical, especially for the insides of containers. Simply pour glaze into the pot and swirl it around as you pour it out — and the job is finished. To pour glaze over the outside is not that simple. The thickness should be carefully watched. *Dipping* a pot into glaze is the easiest method of all and one of the most successful. However, a large quantity of glaze is always needed for this technique. *Spraying* a glaze requires a spray gun and a compressor or blower. A vacuum cleaner with a spray-gun attachment can be used, even a hand-operated flit-gun can be drafted into service for spraying glaze.

All spraying should be done either in a well ventilated room or out-of-doors; it will take practice to do it well and efficiently. (A beginner should supplement instruction in this book with more extensive information from other sources dealing with glazing and finishing; several titles are listed on page 158 under "References for the Beginner.")

A pot treated on the outside with a texture that is beautiful or important to the piece should be preserved as it is or enhanced only with great subtlety. Most of the time pots with beautiful clay textures are best left without a glaze surface.

Small pots or shallow containers such as plates are attractive with a glaze used over a textured surface. But it must be a transparent colored glaze on a light colored clay, or a *translucent glaze on a dark colored clay*. An opaque glaze can cover up a handsome clay texture and turn a good pot into one without character.

STAINING

Texture in clay can be enhanced by careful staining. On gray, buff or light red firing clays a dark stain, generally some shade of brown, may be used. Black is a second choice, with gray-green or gray-blue a dubious third.

Pots may be stained after they are bisque fired. If stains are applied to leather-hard or dry greenware, the moisture of the stain can cause damage. (When the surface of the texture is wiped clean, the sharpness or crispness of the texture will be destroyed.)

When stain is applied to a textured surface, it should be a *very thin stain, heavily applied*. The stain should cover every depression in the clay. It never appears convincing to stain only the high points of a textured surface. After a textured surface is thoroughly colored, the high points should be wiped clean, or nearly clean, leaving the original clay color dominant. The stain intensifies the texture.

For best results, pots should be bisque fired first. Next, the pots should be glazed on the inside. If glaze dribbles down the outside of the form, it can be brushed or sponged off the textured clay surfaces and depressions. Now, the *outside* surface may be stained. Wipe off the stain carefully and thoroughly, using your bare hands or a moist sponge. Then rub it with the palm of your hand. If too much color is wiped off, add more color, then wipe the surface clean again.

Strive to leave the deepest texture depressions filled with color. Tint the medium surface lightly, and wipe the highest points of the texture completely clean of color or stain. A blotchy surface is not satisfactory.

If a pot is to be partially glazed on the outside — the neck of a bottle or the lip of a bowl, for example — the following procedure is good: Glaze the inside of the pot and wipe the outside surface clean. Next, stain the outside clay texture, and wipe and rub it carefully to bring out its true qualities. Then, with a liquid wax emulsion (a liquid floor wax or wax-resist for pottery), wax all the outside surface that is to remain free of glaze. Stir very thoroughly the glaze you are going to use. Now dip the top edge of the pot in the glaze immediately after stirring. If glaze dribbles over the waxed area it can be lifted off with a wet sponge, but, again, this should be done immediately. Glaze applied to areas where you want it to go should be fairly thick. It should stop at a definite line in a clean heavy *roll*. If the glaze tapers off to a thin, ragged line, the glazing job will be inferior.

Shiny glazes or waxy mat glazes are best for the insides of all pots. Mat glazes stain easily and are hard to clean. Used on the insides of containers for food, they are unpleasant to the touch and when scraped with a metal spoon, grate on the ears. A spoon scraped across a mat glaze may also leave a dark mark that is difficult to remove.

Mat glazes, however, are excellent for the outsides of pots, especially pots not used for serving food. They are fine for large pots, or for pots with forms that are strongly textured, modeled or quite "busy." If a shiny glaze is used on an intricate surface pattern, however, it creates a glitter effect with innumerable highlights set off by small shadows. It is so eye-catching as to make the form secondary in importance — precisely the opposite of what a potter usually strives for in a finished surface.

The glaze used on the inside of a pot should generally be a shade lighter than that used on the outside. It is also quite satisfactory, however, to use the same glaze on the inside and the outside. If two glaze colors are used on the same pot, one inside and the other outside, avoid complementary colors, such as yellow and violet, red and green, blue and orange. Complementary colors are striking on posters, but disturbing to live with. A white glaze on the inside of a pot is always satisfactory.

Stoneware fired in a reduction atmosphere seems to give the very best appearance to that clay. A cone 8 to 10 firing is excellent, although a cone 6 to 7 reduction firing is also good.

One of the most beautiful stains for stoneware clay fired in reduction is made from Barnard Clay. It is mixed with water until it is quite thin and closely approximates muddy water. This thin Barnard Clay slip may be sponged or sprayed onto a bisque pot, then wiped off carefully to give a thin tint to the clay. A thick coating will give an appearance similar to a black stove pipe or black cast iron. This black color adds richness to the deepest depressions of a texture. A medium coating of Barnard Clay slip produces a good toasted brown color, whereas a thick coat of the same slip makes a beautiful burnt orange color.

Thin coatings of Barnard Clay slip are satisfactory for a cone 05 or 06 oxidation firing, but it has the appearance of chocolate when glazed. A cone 4 or 5 oxidation firing improves the appearance, but for the lower firings (cones 05 or 06) it would be better to mix 25 to 35 per cent of a *frit* with the Barnard Clay slip. For cones 4 and 5, 15 to 25 per cent of a frit added improves the appearance and makes the stain appear to be a more integral part of the clay.

It is also a good idea to use red iron oxide and water, instead of Barnard Clay, to thinly coat textured clay. This mixture should be treated exactly like Barnard Clay. The final appearance is almost the same and nearly as good as that obtained with Barnard Clay. Glaze stains or underglazes with 10 or 15 per cent frit added to them and mixed with water can be used for staining clay in the same way as that described for Barnard Clay. Black underglaze is quite good as a stain especially on white clay. Browns are satisfactory and some gray-blues and gray-greens also work well.

Dark red clays with textured surfaces are more difficult to treat in a way that will further enhance the surface. One material that has interesting possibilities, however — if used correctly — is *kiln wash* (a mixture of 50 per cent fine flint and 50 per cent China clay). Make the kiln wash very thin with water. Sponge a coat over the dark red clay, then wipe the surface clean. The thickest layer of kiln wash — which is still quite thin — will remain in the deepest depressions of the texture. The tips of the texture should be wiped or sponged clean of the wash. In a cone 8 or 10 reduction firing, the depressions in the texture should become an ivory white or buff color; other areas of the dark red clay body will be an orange bisque color, and the high points should be a rich, dark rust shade. This is almost the reverse result produced by using Barnard Clay slip on buff clay at cones 8 to 10 in a reduction atmosphere.

Here is another way of making a material that should produce a good finish for textured red clay fired high: Use a cone 04 talc white casting body to make a small amount of thin clay slip. Apply it to the bisque-fired red clay body in the same manner described for kiln wash application.

Dark brown or red clay bodies fired in oxidation or reduction can take a glaze on a textured surface with excellent results. The glaze should be translucent, neither clear nor opaque. Not all translucent glazes are good; several should be tested in advance on textured surfaces. It is important to apply the glaze correctly, according to the following method, which differs from the usual manner of glazing:

Dip a sponge into the glaze and sponge it onto the bisque pot. Now dip your hand in the glaze and rub over the pot to fill the depressions. Wet your hand with water over and over again, each time rubbing the pot. Try to keep the glaze packed in the depressions of the texture, while you rub it off the high points. When the pot is fired, the depressions should be filled with a nearly opaque layer of glaze, while the tips of the texture will be exposed clay of a dark, rich color. Very light colored glazes or white glazes are best to use for this technique.

For stoneware temperatures in an oxidation firing there is an unusual method of firing a glaze that should produce excellent results. To test it, try the "Tizzy" glaze or the B glaze described in the following chapter. These are cone 05 or 06 glazes; they should be kept rather thin when applied to the bisque pot, then fired to cone 5 or 6 or on up to cone 10. If the layer of glaze is kept thin, it will run *just freely enough* to fill the depressions in the texture and run off the high points. These glazes are opaque at cones 05 to 06, but translucent at cone 5 or higher. Light colored glazes over dark clay give attractive results. There are many low-fire glazes and low-fire fritted glazes that will work well at a high temperature fire.

Colors will be limited, of course, for many low-fired colors disappear at high temperatures. Copper, cobalt and manganese colors will not disappear, however, and a tin vanadium yellow should hold half of its coloring power, as will the chrome greens.

Most of the pots illustrated were fired to cone 10 in a reduction atmosphere. Some of the glaze recipes chosen for them are found in the following chapter.

17. GLAZE RECIPES

Glaze recipes are somewhat fickle. Subtle and mysterious factors will cause a familiar glaze to work well for one potter and poorly for another, or to work well in one *area* and not in another. One has to experiment with glazes — perhaps even alter the recipes slightly or adjust the firing — to obtain the most satisfactory results.

Because of the unpredictable nature of glazes, opening the kiln is an exciting and rewarding experience, always full of surprises. There will be, of course, a certain percentage of failures, but just enough to challenge one to try again and, perhaps, the next time "win the jackpot."

The following glaze recipes are the results of over thirty years of experimentation, of trial and error. There has been a gradual deletion of some glazes, leaving only those with the most latitude, capable of producing the handsomest and most interesting effects. While most of the glazes described here should work very well for you, keep in mind that it is always wise to test them before final use to discover the glazes you find most appealing. Selection of glazes, as with most things, is largely a matter of personal taste.

Glazes To Be Fired in a Reduction Atmosphere at Cone 10

G MAT 3 WHITE (Figure 186)
CONES 10 AND 11
This is an excellent glaze with mottled effects. It is dry at cone 9½ when thin, and waxy when thick and fired at cone 11. It is good in an oxidation atmosphere, especially on porcelain.

	Grams
Feldspar	1561
Whiting	266
Zinc oxide	241
Barium carbonate	631
Ball clay	300
Rutile	60

For colors add the following:

		Grams
Green	Copper carbonate	40
Turquoise	Copper carbonate	22
Brown	Red iron oxide	150
Tan	Red iron oxide	60
Olive green	{ Chromium oxide	7
	{ Black nickel oxide	45

Cobalt blue	Cobalt oxide	40
Yellow green	Yellow green G.S. #309	300
	(B. F. Drakenfeld Co.)	
Green brown	{ Copper carbonate	8
mottled	{ Red iron oxide	76

MG 2 WHITE MAT (Figure 187)
CONES 10 AND 11

This is a stiff, rather opaque, waxy glaze excellent for the majolica or wax-resist technique.

	Grams
Soda feldspar	1284
Ball clay	357
Gerstley borate	568
Dolomite	416
Talc	932
Flint	1200

For colors add the following:

		Grams
Pale turquoise	Blue green G.S. #100	24
	(Pemco Corp.)	
Turquoise	Blue green G.S. #100	36
	(Pemco Corp.)	
Blue gray	Black U.G. #1117	48
Brown	{ Green chromium oxide	15
	{ Red iron oxide	24
Yellow green	Red iron oxide	96

STONY WHITE MAT   CONE 10

This is a dull mat, very good for some effects.

	Grams
Feldspar	1670
Dolomite	550
Whiting	100
Kaolin	770
Talc	300
Granular ilmenite	100

For colors add the following:

		Grams
Black	Black U.G. #1786	160
Gray	Black U.G. #1117	35
Tan	{ Red iron oxide	70
	{ Black nickel oxide	53
Violet blue	Cobalt oxide	18

K.C.N.S.T. OPAQUE SATIN IRON GLAZE
CONES 8 TO 10

This glaze is khaki brown where it is thin, and a deep brown-black where it is thick. Sometimes it has iron crystals in it that glisten.

	Grams
Feldspar	1839
Whiting	225
Kaolin	147
Flint	744
Red iron oxide	300

BRIGHT BROWN-BLACK SHINY OPAQUE
GLAZE (Figure 188)   CONE 10

	Grams
Feldspar	1647
Whiting	620
Zinc oxide	81
Kaolin	480
Flint	828
Red iron oxide	356

WAXY MAT GLAZE (Figure 189)
CONES 9 TO 10

A beautiful semi-mat glaze, it is translucent when used thin or fired to cone 11. It is also excellent in an oxidation atmosphere.

	Grams
Feldspar	1230
Gerstley borate	360
Dolomite	210
Talc	450
Kaolin	150
Flint	600

For a beautiful speckled effect add 20 grams of granular magnetite or ilmenite. For colors add the following:

		Grams
Turquoise	{ Black U.G. #1786	30
	{ Black nickel oxide	45
	{ Magnetite	20
Pale blue	Turquoise G.S. #500	150
	(Harshaw Company)	
Oatmeal	Powdered ilmenite	65
Black	Black G.S. #1117	90
Gray	Black G.S. #1117	24
Strong blue green	Blue green G.S. #100	30
	(Pemco Corp.)	
Brown	Red iron oxide	150

CHUN GLAZE (Figures 190, 191, 192) SHINY,

COLORLESS AND TRANSPARENT
CONES 9 TO 10

This is an excellent all-purpose glaze. It is clear at cone 11 and translucent at cone 9. It has tin oxide to increase the effects of a reduction glaze when there is enough reduction. If the kiln is not reduced heavily enough, the glaze will be opaque. Tin oxide may be omitted for a clear glaze in oxidation.

	Grams
Feldspar	1440
Kaolin	50
Flint	900
Whiting	90
Gerstley borate	300
Dolomite	300
Zinc oxide	60
Barium carbonate	150
Tin oxide	90

For colors add the following:

		Grams
Opaque white	Ultrox	339
Celadon	Red iron oxide	68
Dark celadon	Red iron oxide	136
Brown	Red iron oxide	204
Blue	Red iron oxide	40
	Cobalt blue	20
Copper red	Copper carbonate	17
Mottled blue	Rutile	170
	Copper carbonate	17
Chrome green	Green chromium oxide	51
Pale chrome blue	Chromium oxide	51
	Gerstley borate	678

PM 5 EGGSHELL MAT   CONE 10

	Grams
Feldspar	1512
Dolomite	504
Whiting	84
Kaolin	700

For colors add the following:

		Grams
Tan	Red iron oxide	70
Pale violet blue	Cobalt oxide	7
Gray	Manganese dioxide	140

MOTTLED BLUE   CONE 10

	Grams
Barium carbonate	270

Flint	90
Kaolin	90
Feldspar	500
Dolomite	40
Copper carbonate	39

TRANSPARENT GRAY MAT   CONE 10

This is as transparent as a good mat will be. It works well over engobes and is especially effective with cobalt oxide painted over or under it.

	Grams
Dolomite	558
Nepheline syenite	1350
Whiting	300
Kaolin	822
Flint	460
Opax	110
Zinc oxide	80

CELADON (GREEN BLUE)   CONE 10

This is a good, dependable celadon.

	Grams
Feldspar	556
Whiting	400
Kaolin	407
Flint	672
Red iron oxide	20

CHOY BLUE CELADON (Figure 193) CONE 10

	Grams
Feldspar	1226
Whiting	150
Kaolin	98
Flint	496
Barium carbonate	400
Red iron oxide	50

MC 532A TURQUOISE   CONES 8 TO 10

This is an unusual, beautiful copper blue mat. It is also excellent in an oxidation atmosphere.

	Grams
Barium carbonate	600
Nepheline syenite	1300
Kaolin	140
Flint	160
Lithium carbonate	40
Copper carbonate	100

Glazes To Be Fired in an Oxidizing Atmosphere at Cone 5

These glazes should work well from cones 4 to 6, depending on the firing of the kiln and how you prefer your glazes finished.

#16 GLAZE

This is an excellent transparent glaze unusually good for this temperature range. The opaque colors, made opaque with 7 per cent of tin oxide, are good but not unusual.

	Grams
Feldspar	868.0
Flint	487.0
Kaolin	19.6
Gerstley borate	406.0
Whiting	29.6
Zinc oxide	63.2
Barium	126.6

For colors add the following:

		Grams
Opaque cream	Rutile	130
Opaque white	Tin oxide	140
Emerald green	Copper carbonate	60
	Rutile	22
Olive green	Copper carbonate	40
	Red iron oxide	50
	Rutile	15
Spring green	Copper carbonate	30
	Tin vanadium yellow G.S.	50
	Rutile	15
Opal blue	Cobalt oxide	5
	Rutile	60
Topaz yellow	Red iron oxide	40
	Manganese dioxide	40
	Rutile	20
Amythyst	Manganese dioxide	100
	Rutile	20
Blue green	Copper oxide	30
	Cobalt oxide	5
Sky blue	Turquoise G.S. #500 (Harshaw Company)	120
Gold translucent	Tin vanadium yellow U.G. (Harshaw Company)	104
Red brown opaque	Orange brown U.G. #501 (B. F. Drakenfeld Co.)	120

GIB MAT DRY IVORY WHITE (Figure 194) CONE 5

	Grams
Nepheline syenite	1182
Whiting	256
Zinc oxide	226
Kaolin	392
Flint	34

For colors add the following:

		Grams
Yellow	Tin vanadium yellow U.G.	104
Dark gray	Copper carbonate	31
	Cobalt oxide	5
Tan	Red iron oxide	41
	Copper carbonate	31
Pale blue	Cobalt oxide	5
	Rutile	62
Green	Copper carbonate	31
	Tin vanadium U.G. or G.S.	52

DARK ALBANY BROWN GLOSSY TRANSPARENT (Figure 194)   CONE 5

By itself this is a good, plain brown glaze, but try putting a good layer of Gib Mat Ivory White over this for an unusual bubbly or mottled effect. The thickness of each glaze controls the mottled effect.

	Grams
Albany clay	2503
Cornwall stone	96
Ball clay	40
Flint	93
Whiting	34
Zinc oxide	17
Red lead	214

For a darker color add 5 per cent of red iron oxide. For a brown-black, add 5 per cent of red iron oxide and 1 per cent of cobalt oxide.

MC 532A TURQUOISE   CONE 5

This is a heavenly copper blue mat.

	Grams
Barium carbonate	600
Nepheline syenite	1350
Ball clay	140
Flint	160

Copper carbonate	70
Lithium carbonate	70

BC DRY MAT CONE 5

This is a lead glaze that is excellent for red clays and to put over some engobes. Use a thin application.

	Grams
White lead	960
Whiting	300
Kaolin	300
Feldspar	400
Flint	100
Tin oxide	160

For colors add the following:

		Grams
Charcoal	Red iron oxide	40
	Manganese oxide	40
Russet	Red iron oxide	42
	Tin oxide	60
Verde gris	Red iron oxide	42
	Copper carbonate	31
Mist	Manganese dioxide	35
	Cobalt oxide	4
	Red iron oxide	4
Ivory	Rutile	15
	Red iron oxide	5

COLEMENITE GLOSSY GLAZE CONE 5

This glaze should give beautiful colors, especially the blues and greens.

	Grams
Frit 3134	760
(Ferro Corp.)	
Feldspar	1047
Whiting	168
Gerstley borate	152
Ball clay	109
Flint	760

For color add the following:

		Grams
Turquoise	Copper carbonate	90
Gray blue	Iron chromate	90
Tan	Milled ilmenite	90
Blue green	Copper carbonate	90
	Cobalt oxide	15

METALLIC BLACK GLOSSY CONE 5

This glaze is good by itself or over other glazes to give mottling and specks.

	Grams
Kaolin	95
Feldspar	1526
Whiting	106
Gerstley borate	208
Copper carbonate	80
Manganese dioxide	80
Cobalt oxide	40

BI MAT CONES 2 TO 5

	Grams
White lead	676
Whiting	419
Feldspar	936
Kaolin	387
Calcined clay	141
Zinc oxide	169
Flint	272

For colors add the following:

		Grams
Pink	Ruby red U.G.	210
Yellow	Yellow U.G. #5100	150
	(Harshaw Company)	
Yellow green	Yellow U.G. #5100	150
	(Harshaw Company)	
	Copper carbonate	30
Green	Copper carbonate	90
Plum	Manganese dioxide	120
	Chinese blue U.G.	60
Black	Cobalt oxide	60
	Iron oxide	150
	Calcined clay	240
Mullen green	Copper carbonate	60
	Red iron oxide	60

A MAT SPECKLED CONE 5

	Grams
Feldspar	664
White lead	300
Dolomite	214
Whiting	118
Kaolin	295
Flint	100
Albany clay slip	280
Tin oxide	140

After the glaze is mixed, add 30 grams of granular magnetite or ilmenite and stir it by hand.

LA MAT (Figure 194)   CONES 5 AND 6

An excellent mat, especially for a variety of colors.

	Grams
Feldspar	1548
Flint	168
Whiting	564
Zinc oxide	258
Kaolin	462

For colors add the following:

		Grams
Turquoise	Copper carbonate	15
Yellow	Yellow G.S. #1500 (Harshaw Company)	150
Red brown	Red brown U.G. #123 (O. Hommel Co.)	150
Blue	Turquoise blue G.S. #500 (Harshaw Company)	150
Green	Black copper oxide	75
Black	Red iron oxide	150
	Cobalt oxide	30
Violet brown	Manganese dioxide	60
	Rutile	90
Blue green	Black copper oxide	45
	Turquoise blue G.S. #500 (Harshaw Company)	150
Gray	Black copper oxide	45
	Rutile	90
	Cobalt oxide	30

SATIN MAT   CONE 5

	Grams
White lead	1177.5
Whiting	290.4
Feldspar	494.7
Ball clay	795.3
Flint	239.1

Glazes To Be Fired in an Oxidizing Atmosphere at Cones 08 to 04 but Also as High as Cone 10 for Unusual but Beautiful Results

The following four glazes are excellent for low-fired earthenware, cones 08 to 04. They are also excellent glazes for any temperature up to cone 10 in an oxidation firing. When they are applied thin, there is no excessive running; the quality of the clay shows through the glaze beautifully.

"TIZZY" GLAZE (Figures 196, 197)
CONES 08 TO 10

	Grams
Flint	463
White lead	1500
Feldspar	300
Kaolin	420
Frit 3134 (Ferro Corp.)	570

For a translucent glaze, add 162 grams of tin oxide. For an opaque glaze, add 300 grams of tin oxide. The glaze is not effective as a transparent glaze; some tin oxide should be added.

For colors add the following:

		Grams
Black	Black U.G.	182
Light turquoise	Copper carbonate	73
Rust	Black iron oxide	146
Chinese blue	Chinese blue U.G.	182
Cobalt blue	Cobalt oxide	73
Blue green	Copper carbonate	109
	Cobalt oxide	9
Green	Copper carbonate	182
Pale blue	Turquoise blue G.S. #500 (Harshaw Company)	182

"B" GLAZE   CONES 08 TO 10 OXIDATION

When this glaze is fired from cones 08 to 04, it is an opaque satin mat. At cones 4 and 5 it has a curdled texture; from cones 8 to 10, applied thin, it brings out all the impurities in the clay and is translucent:

	Grams
Frit #33 (O. Hommel Co.)	1800
Ball clay	300
Magnesium zirconium silicate	600
Feldspar	300

For colors add the following:

		Grams
Blue	Cobalt oxide	30
Chinese blue	Chinese blue U.G.	60

Green	Copper oxide	60
Turquoise	Copper carbonate	30
Yellow	Tin vanadium yellow U.G.	150

GROUND GLASS GLAZE
CONES 08 TO 10 OXIDATION

As a transparent glossy glaze, this is excellent for underglaze painting fired to cone 07. When 7 per cent of tin oxide is added to make it opaque, it is an excellent glaze upon which to paint with underglazes for majolica ware. To color the glaze for 07 firing, most underglazes give excellent colors. For higher firing, 2 per cent or 3 per cent of tin oxide gives best results.

	Grams
Ground glass (or cullet)	250
White lead	250
Frit #25	250
(O. Hommel Co.)	
China clay	150

Only a few colors can be used when the glaze is fired high. They are as follows:

		Grams
Blue	Cobalt oxide	27
Green	Copper oxide	54
Yellow	Tin vanadium yellow U.G.	60
Brown	Red iron oxide	135

GLAZE #138-0 OPAQUE SHINING GLAZE
CONES 08 TO 10 OXIDATION

This is a dependable, opaque, shiny glaze that takes most colors well. When applied thin it can be fired as high as cone 10 in oxidation.

	Grams
Frit #24	210
(O. Hommel Co.)	
Kaolin	30
Litharage	16
Zircopax	14
Magnesium zirconium silicate	30

For colors add the following:

		Grams
Dark blue	Cobalt oxide	30
Light blue	Chinese blue U.G.	120
Turquoise	Copper carbonate	60
Green	Copper oxide	120

Violet brown or Gray violet	Manganese dioxide	120
Yellow	Tin vanadium yellow U.G.	170

Glazes To Be Fired in an Oxidizing Atmosphere at Cones 08 to 04

GLAZE J/S MAT   CONES 03 TO 05

This is an excellent mat that will give good results over some engobes. It has some pleasing color effects.

	Grams
White lead	387
Whiting	60
Zinc oxide	36
Feldspar	252
Calcined kaolin	132
Flint	54

For color add the following:

		Grams
Black	Manganese dioxide	30
	Copper oxide	45
	Cobalt blue	51
Transparent green	Copper carbonate	90
Spring morning	Lead chromate	30
	Victoria green U.G.	5
Cypress	Tin oxide	20
	Copper oxide	120
French green	French green U.G.	90
Opaque green	Tin oxide	210
	Lead chromate	30
	Copper carbonate	30
Meadow green	Tin oxide	210
	Lead chromate	30
	Copper carbonate	30
Azure blue	King's blue U.G.	15
Chinese blue	Cobalt oxide	3
Golden brown	Tin oxide	180
	Red iron oxide	270
Mystery	Nickel oxide	45
Autumn	Lead chromate	120
Yellow	Tin oxide	182
	Tin vanadium yellow U.G.	182
Old wine	Manganese dioxide	45

METALLIC BLACK GLAZE SHINY
CONES 08 TO 04

By itself, this is a very lustrous black. It is excellent

sprayed lightly or in a medium layer over other glazes. Over an opaque white, it gives an interesting texture of blues, violets and grays.

	Grams
White lead	930
Whiting	60
Feldspar	336
Zinc oxide	96
Kaolin	66
Flint	600
Black copper oxide	48
Manganese dioxide	84

GRAY BLUE RUTILE GLAZE MAT
CONES 08 TO 04

This is a rough, rather unpleasant mat by itself, but it is excellent applied over other glazes, especially shiny, opaque glazes. Other colors may be used instead of cobalt oxide.

	Grams
White lead	1423.8
Feldspar	222.7
Flint	255.2
Rutile	136.4
Cobalt oxide	36.0

3/3 MAT IVORY   CONES 05 TO 04

This is a rough ivory colored mat glaze. Some colors can be added, but they are limited in effect. This glaze is excellent over dark red and brown clays at cone 04.

	Grams
White lead	1475
Feldspar	475
Barium carbonate	225
Kaolin	100
Cornish stone	100

V/V MAT   CONES 07 TO 03

This is a smooth, translucent mat. It is good over engobes. Color can be added.

	Grams
White lead	1800
Feldspar	300
Zinc oxide	588
Kaolin	240
Flint	600

MC 1 TURQUOISE   CONES 07 TO 05

	Grams
Gerstley borate	82.4
Cryolite	8.4
Whiting	25.0
Feldspar	87.5
Talc	10.4
Kaolin	26.0
Flint	145.5
White lead	38.2
Copper carbonate	4.0

MC 2 TURQUOISE SHINY   CONES 05 TO 03

	Grams
Feldspar	119.2
Gerstley borate	82.4
Zinc oxide	24.3
Barium carbonate	19.7
Kaolin	13.9
Flint	96.2
Whiting	3.5
Copper carbonate	4.0

MC 4 MAT   CONES 05 TO 03

	Grams
Feldspar	90.8
Gerstley borate	51.5
Barium carbonate	9.4
Flint	60.0
Whiting	27.0

047 OPAQUE RED SHINY   CONES 05 TO 03

This glaze should give an excellent red with any chrome-tin red color. Not all glazes give good strong reds. This one will.

	Grams
White lead	40.6
Whiting	8.0
Kaolin	7.0
Flint	18.0
Frit 3134	23.0
(Ferro Corp.)	
Tin oxide	8.0
Red glaze stains or	
underglazes	6.0

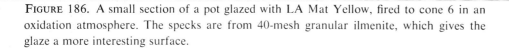

FIGURE 186. A small section of a pot glazed with LA Mat Yellow, fired to cone 6 in an oxidation atmosphere. The specks are from 40-mesh granular ilmenite, which gives the glaze a more interesting surface.

FIGURE 187. This detail of a glazed pot shows MG2 Turquoise glaze with 3 per cent of 40-mesh granular ilmenite added. The glaze was fired to cone 10 in a reduction atmosphere. When the glaze is thick and fired high enough to flux the ilmenite in a reduction atmosphere, the specks of ilmenite enlarge, thus creating a very nice pattern of brown on turquoise blue.

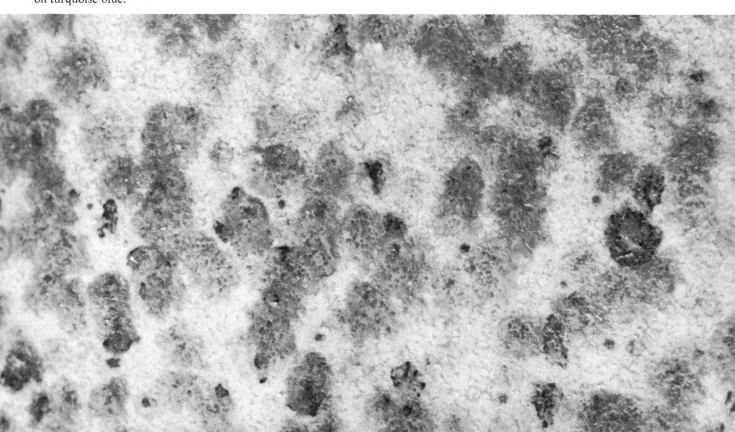

FIGURE 188. In this area of a pot glazed with Green G Mat 3 glaze, the surface of the glaze is mottled. This is due to the way in which the glaze boiled when it fused. The darker areas are a green black, the light areas turquoise blue. The thickness of the glaze and the firing alter the G Mat 3 glazes so that the results are always surprising, and generally most pleasing. The glaze was fired to cone 10 in a reduction atmosphere.

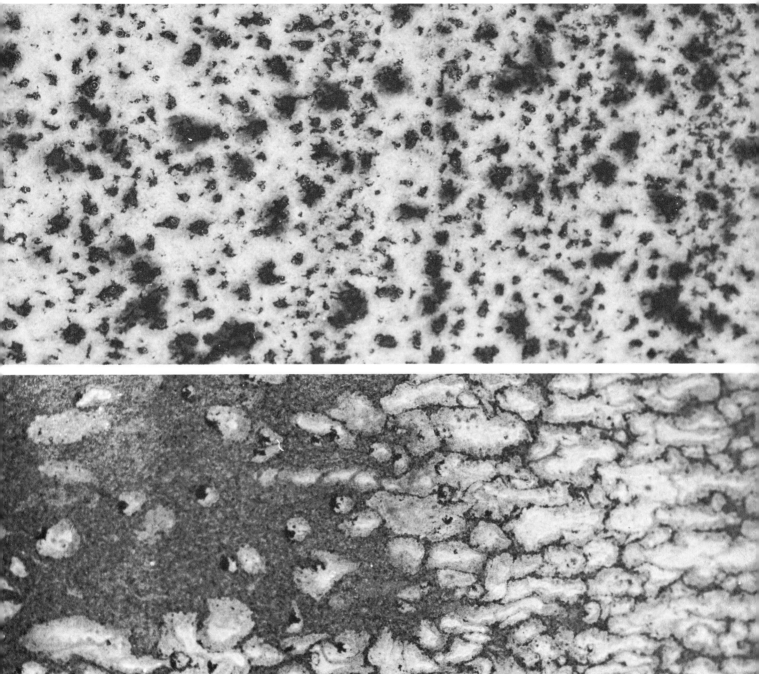

FIGURE 189. The glaze in this detail of a pot is Choy Blue Celadon fired to cone 10 in a reduction atmosphere. The pot is porcelain; the glaze crazes or crackles on this body. The glaze is a beautiful turquoise green because of the 2 per cent iron oxide added. The white clay under the transparent glaze makes the color clearer and more delicate.

149

FIGURE 190. This is a section of a buff clay pot fired to cone 10 in a reduction atmosphere. It is Chun Celadon color with 2 per cent iron oxide to make it a celadon, or grayed blue-green color. The glaze is shiny and transparent. It is applied thickly and not over-fired, and therefore is full of minute bubbles that refract the light, giving a richer quality than a clear, bubble-free glaze would have.

FIGURE 191. This detail of a glazed area on a pot shows a mottled effect caused by the first thick layer of Bright Brown Black glaze bubbling through a second, thick layer of opaque white Chun glaze. The thickness of each glaze affects the mottled pattern that developed in the cone 10 firing.

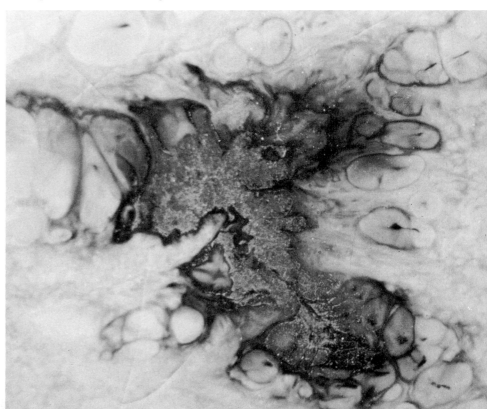

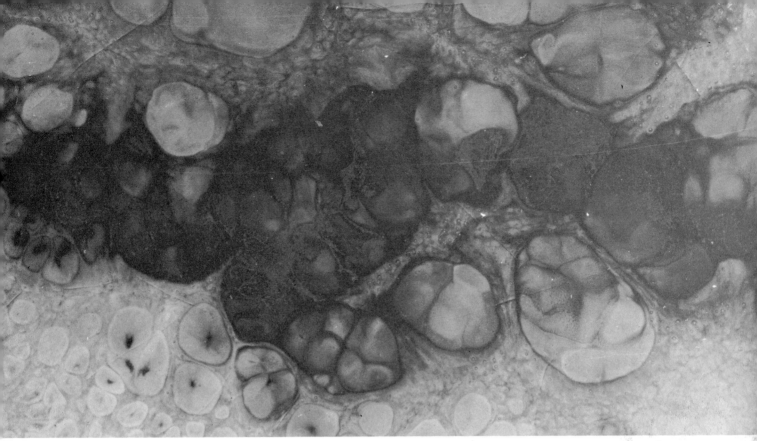

FIGURE 192. This is a detail of a glaze in the bottom of a plate fired to cone 10 in a reduction atmosphere. It is transparent blue Chun over opaque white Chun with 15 per cent of gerstley borate added to the glaze. The glaze boils and flows to create these accidental patterns that are unusual and fascinating.

FIGURE 193. This detail of a glaze on the bottom of a plate is opaque Chun glaze with 15 per cent gerstley borate added to it to make it bubble and boil. The dark area shows the effect of a brush stroke of red iron oxide applied to the surface. This same glaze on a vertical surface is quite different. The glaze was fired to cone 10 in a reduction atmosphere.

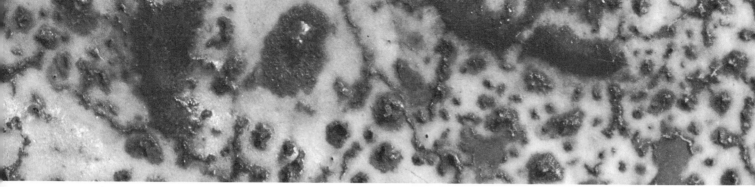

FIGURE 194. Detail of a small section of a pot first glazed thickly with Dark Brown Albany Slip glaze, then thickly glazed with colorless Gib Mat glaze. The dark glaze is brown, the light one, a cream color. The Albany Slip glaze always bubbles through the Gib Mat glaze. The glaze will crawl, blister or bubble, or just become mottled, but always, depending on the thickness of the glaze and the firing, producing an unexpected, intriguing effect.

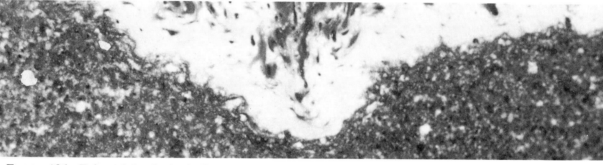

FIGURE 195. A small section of a pot glazed with Black Waxy glaze, then dipped into Oatmeal Waxy glaze. When the glaze is fired, it boils and bubbles to create the mottled effect seen here, or a variation of it, depending on the thickness of the glazes and the firing. This pot was fired to cone 9½ in a reduction atmosphere.

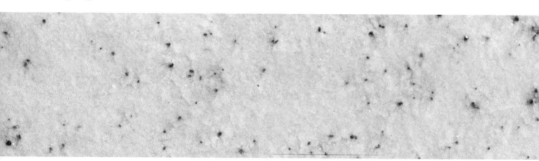

FIGURE 196. Enlarged detail of a buff clay pot glazed with blue transparent Tizzy glaze and fired to cone 5. Notice how the clay impurities bleed through the glaze at medium thickness.

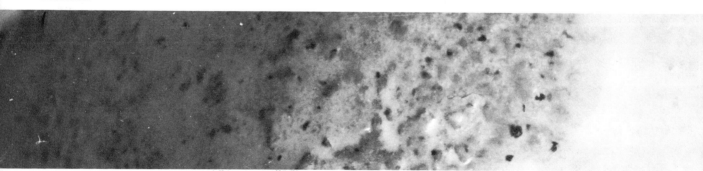

FIGURE 197. Detail of a red clay pot glazed with translucent white Tizzy glaze fired to cone 8 in oxidation. Notice the dark red clay dominating, although partially covered with white, to produce a beautiful rust red.

18. TERRA SIGILLATA

Terra Sigillata is an ancient method of finishing pottery. While a careful analysis of many types of primitive ceramics reveals the use of this method, it is generally acknowledged that the early Romans surpassed everyone in its skillful application. In some ways Terra Sigillata resembles an engobe. It is distinguished by an almost glaze-like density, satin polish, and an excellent hardness. It generally fires to a rich iron-red color.

To make the standard Terra Sigillata, obtain some ordinary surface clay, which is nearly always a red color when fired. The more plastic and finely ground the clay is, the better it is for making this material. Dry the clay out and crush it. Then soak it in water, without stirring, for about one hour. After this hour-long soaking, stir it thoroughly, and add more water if necessary to make a soupy liquid. Then screen it through a 100-mesh screen to remove particles of leaves, grass, roots and sand. If this screened clay is ground in a ball mill for a day or two, it will improve the material, but this is not mandatory.

Deflocculate the clay slip. Add "Calgon," the same powder used in washing machines, from 0.15 per cent to 0.30 per cent, to the slip. Or, better still, use sodium hydroxide. The slip should be extremely thin. For best results the specific gravity of the slip should be 1.2, which in appearance approximates muddy water.

Let the mixture settle overnight. If the slip is really good, there will be very little clear water on top. The heaviest particles will sink to the bottom of the container. Siphon off the top half of the muddy water — *this is your Terra Sigillata*. Throw away the bottom half of the mixture.

Take your dry, unfired pot and dip it into the Terra Sigillata *once*. The pot can be wet-sprayed lightly, if dipping is impractical. As the pot dries it takes on a silken sheen; this indicates good material and good application. It can now be rubbed gently with the palm of the hand to give it a polish. The very small, almost colloidal, clay disklets lie flat, overlapping one another, to produce a silken sheen. This tissue-paper-thin layer of extremely fine clay is quite hard and dense.

The ware can be fired *once*. This standard Terra Sigillata is best when fired from cone 06 to cone 04. For a higher-fired ware and a white color, make it out of Ball clay, then fire it to cones 5 or 6. If China clay is used, the final firing should be at cone 10. It is possible to add coloring oxides to the slip, but they should be ground thoroughly.

Terra Sigillata is an excellent finish for pottery that has a textured surface. Cover the outside of a textured pot with an extremely thin coating of Terra Sigillata; let it dry, then take a wet sponge and wipe off the slip from the high points of the texture. Bisque fire the pot, then glaze the inside, perhaps also the top or lip outside, and fire it again to the most suitable temperature. The results should be both beautiful and unusual.

GLOSSARY OF TERMS

Absorption. Taking up or soaking up water into the pores of a material such as clay or plaster of paris.

Albany slip. A natural clay that melts into a brown glass at fairly low temperatures. If a layer of Albany Clay slip is put onto a form made of high firing clay and the form is fired to 2200°F. or higher, the Albany Clay slip will turn into a shiny brown glaze on the high-fired form. Albany Clay slip is silt from the Hudson River near Albany, New York. River silts from other locations sometimes give similar results.

Alumina. Aluminum oxide, Al_2O_3. A major ingredient found in all clays, alumina is used in nearly all glazes. It is introduced into glazes by means of kaolin. Increasing the kaolin content helps to keep glazes from running.

Ball clay. A type of sedimentary clay that is very plastic and fine grained. Although the raw clay is usually dark in color, it fires to a white or cream color.

Bat, plaster. Any plaster of paris slab or disk. Bats are used to support clay work — either hand-built or wheel-thrown — in progress. Bats are also used to absorb water from clay in order to make soft clay firm enough to work with.

Batch. A mixture of weighed or measured materials or ingredients, such as a glaze batch, a batch for an engobe or a clay body.

Bentonite. An extremely plastic clay of volcanic origin. It is used only in small amounts and must be mixed with other ingredients in dry form before it can be used. The addition of 1 or 2 per cent of bentonite will increase the plasticity of a clay. It can also be used to keep glaze materials in suspension.

Bisque or biscuit. Pottery that has been fired but not glazed. A bisque firing is generally a low fire (Cone 07) for most art ware. It is usually advisable to bisque fire all ware before it is glazed and fired a second time, in order to mature the glaze.

Black-hard. The condition which a plastic clay or body reaches on drying, when the clay is moist yet hard and rigid and often a darker color than the plastic clay. The point at which the clay is beginning to become dry.

Body or clay body. A mixture or blend of two or more clays and/or clay-like materials designed for a specific type of pottery ware.

Body stain. A specially prepared colorant designed to color pottery clays.

Burning. Baking or firing clay ware in a kiln.

Burnishing. Rubbing moist or leather-hard clay with a smooth pebble, wooden stick or steel tool to polish the surface.

Calcine. To heat a material in a kiln, usually to a moderate temperature, in order to eliminate chemically combined water and expel volatile matter. Clay is frequently calcined.

Casting. The process of forming objects with molds made of plaster or bisque-fired clay. Usually plaster or clay slip is poured into a mold to cast or shape a form.

Ceramics. The art and science of forming objects from earthy material containing silica, with the aid of high-heat treatment.

Chemically combined water. Water which is combined in molecular form with clay. The H_2O in the theoretical formula for clay: $Al_2O_3 \cdot 2\,SiO_2 \cdot 2H_2O$.

China clay. Another name for kaolin or primary clay or residual clay. It fires white, is not very plastic and is quite refractory.

Clay. Theoretically, $Al_2O_3 \cdot 2SiO_2 \cdot 2H_2O$. Fine-grained earthy materials formed by the decomposition of feldspars, containing a considerable amount of the mineral kaolinite which, when combined with water, is plastic enough to be shaped and, when dry, is strong; incandescent heat alters it to a rock-like form.

Cones (pyrometric cones). Tall, slender, three-sided pyramids made of clay and glaze constituents which bend or melt at a given temperature in a kiln. Cones are placed in a kiln where they can be observed from the outside when the kiln is hot and are used as a guide to the finishing or end heat inside. Cones are numbered as a key to their melting point. The numbers begin at 022 (1085° F.), for measuring the lowest temperature, and proceed to higher temperatures through cone 01, cone 1 and on up to cone 42 (3659° F.) Popular temperature ranges are cones 06 to 04 for earthenware, cones 4 and 5 for hard earthenware or soft stoneware, and cones 8 to 10 for stoneware.

Crackle glaze. A decorative network of minute cracks on the surface of a glaze. Crackling results from the fact that the contraction or shrinkage factor of the glaze is slightly greater than that of the clay body.

Crawling. A defect in glazing process in which the glaze gathers in lumps leaving portions of the body exposed. Many glazes when not fired high enough will crawl.

Crazing. The same as crackle except that it is a glaze *defect* and is unwanted and undesirable.

Damp closet. A box, cupboard, closet or room that is kept very humid and unventilated. It is used to store unfinished work so the clay will not dry out.

Damper. A slab of refractory clay that is used to close, or partially close, the flue of a kiln.

Dipping. The application of glaze or engobe to clay ware by immersion. The piece is dipped in the mixture just long enough to cover the desired area with an even coating of glaze or engobe.

Dry-footed ware. Clay ware without glaze on the foot.

Earthenware. All glazed ware with a permeable or porous body, with an absorbency of from 5 to 20 per cent. Usually pottery fired under 2000° F.

Engobe. A clay-like slip (the same as a color clay slip) which is applied to unfired ware or to bisque ware to change the color of the clay body.

Fat clay. A very plastic clay such as Ball clay.

Feldspar. A rock containing Na_2O, K_2O, Al_2O_3 and SiO_2 and sometimes CaO and Li_2O. It is found in granite and melts between 1200° and 1300° C. It is used extensively in clay bodies and glazes. When it loses its alkaline content through decomposition in nature it becomes kaolin and is thus the origin of most potters' clays.

Filler. A clay-like material that is not plastic, such as the flint or silica used in clay bodies to promote drying and to control shrinkage.

Fire. To heat in a kiln to the required temperature.

Fit. The adjustment in the shrinkage of a glaze and the clay it covers.

Flint. Roughly, quartz, silica or silica sand, all terms that apply to the material silica (SiO_2), which is used extensively in both clay bodies and glazes. Without silica we would not have a ceramic product.

Flux. A substance that usually melts at low temperature, thus causing refractory substances to melt into a glaze-like material at lower temperatures and in greater quantity than they would otherwise.

Foot. The base, bottom, legs or ring forming the area that a ceramic piece rests upon.

Frit. Powdered glass made from complete or nearly complete glaze which has been melted, cooled, and pulverized so that it may be used again as a glaze or glaze ingredient. It is used chiefly to make soluble glaze materials insoluble and also to keep lead from being poisonous.

Fuse. To melt under the action of heat.

Glaze. A thin coating of glass. An impervious silicate coating which is developed on clay ware by the fusion under heat of inorganic materials.

Green ware. Pottery that has not been fired.

Grog. Clay that has been fired then crushed to form a coarse, medium-grained or fine sand-like material. Grog can be of any color. It can be added to clay in amounts up to 30 per cent. The addition of grog to clay reduces shrinkage, reduces drying or firing cracks, reduces warping, and enables the potter to use thicker areas of clay without the risk of blowing up the ware in bisque firing. Grog can add a decorative texture to the clay.

Gums. Gums as binders are used to adhere glazes and ceramic colorants to a ceramic surface. They burn out during firing. Gum tragacanth and gum arabic are natural gums. They are excellent but will sour without a preservative. C.M.C. gum, a synthetic, will not sour.

Ilmenite. $TiO_2 \cdot FeO$. A special kind of black sand. Used in granular form, it produces dark specks in glazes. A good quantity to use is 3 per cent.

Impermeable. In pottery this term describes those bodies which have been rendered non-porous or glasslike by vitrifications.

Kaolin. The anglicized form of the Chinese word for China clay. A primary or residual pure clay, Kaolin fires white, withstands high temperature, is not very plastic and is an important constituent of porcelain, china, white clays and most glazes.

Kiln. A furnace or oven for firing pottery. It should be constructed so as to withstand a minimum temperature of 2000° F. It is pronounced "kill."

Leather-hard. The slightly flexible yet firm condition which a plastic clay or body reaches on partially drying.

Mat glaze. A glaze formulated to produce a dull, non-reflecting finish.

Maturity. The temperature or time at which clay ware becomes hard or vitreous enough to have desirable characteristics or when a glaze reaches the point of complete fusion.

Mold. A form, generally made of bisque-fired clay or plaster of paris, which is used to reproduce any number of identical copies of an original design. Various types of molds include slip molds, press molds and hump molds or waste molds.

Muffle. A fire clay wall or box within a kiln where the ware is stacked to protect it from the flames of a gas, wood or oil fuel.

Non-plastic material. Ceramic material that shows no plasticity when mixed with water (for example: sand, grog, flint, feldspar, etc.).

Opacifier. A material added to a transparent or colored transparent glaze to make it opaque. (A transparent glaze becomes opaque white.) The most common opacifiers are tin oxide, titanium and zirconium.

Opalescent glaze. A glaze with a milky, translucent — sometimes bluish — sheen.

Open clays. Porous or sandy-textured clays, clays that are not excessively plastic, or lean, as opposed to fat clays. Open materials are non-plastic materials such as Flint Fire clay, sand and grog.

Oxidation or oxidizing fire. The firing of a kiln in a manner that mixes oxygen with the fuel to produce a clean flame with no soot or smoke and complete combustion. The atmosphere within the kiln contains sufficient oxygen to allow the elements in the clay and glaze to be completely oxidized.

Peephole. A small observation hole in the wall or door of a kiln.

Plasticity. The quality of clay which permits it to be readily shaped into different forms without cracking, crumbling or sagging.

Porosity. The quality of being porous, of being filled with air spaces, of absorbing or soaking up liquid.

Pottery. A loosely used term, often meaning clay pieces of the earthenware type, or a place where clay ware is made.

Pressing. Forming plastic clay against a mold in order to shape it.

Pyrometer. An instrument (*not* a pyrometric cone) used for measuring the temperature in a kiln during firing and cooling. The most common are thermoelectric and optical pyrometers.

Quartz. A common natural mineral, SiO_2, that is the low temperature, stable form of silica.

Raw glaze. A glaze made of ingredients that are insoluble in water and one that does not employ a frit.

Reduction, or reducing fire. In contrast to an oxidizing fire, a reduction fire is a sooty, smoky firing in which the fuel is not completely burned because it does not have enough oxygen. The unburned gasses and the excess of carbon in the kiln atmosphere rob the clay and glaze elements of part of their oxygen content, thus altering or reducing them. This type of firing changes the color of both clay and glaze. Copper red and celadon glazes are typical results of a reduction firing.

Refractory. Having resistance to melting or fusion. Refractory clays such as the clays used to make fire brick, kiln linings and kiln shelves, can withstand high temperatures without melting.

Secondary clays. Clays washed by nature from their source and deposited in the quiet waters of lakes and estuaries. For example: Surface clays, Ball clays, Fire clays.

Shard or sherd. A broken piece of pottery.

Short. The quality of slight plasticity in a clay body.

Silica. SiO_2, oxide of silica. Found abundantly in nature as quartz or flint.

Single fire. A one-step firing in which green ware is glazed and fired to maturity without a preliminary bisque firing. This is a risky procedure, as the ware can crack in glazing, it is hard to handle, it can blow up in firing and ruin many other pieces of ware, and more than the usual number of pieces may have glazes that are pinholed.

Slake. To soak in water.

Slip. A suspension of ceramic materials, either bodies or glazes, in water. Clay slip is water and clay in the consistency of heavy cream.

Slurry. A term describing clay of a soft, paste-like consistency.

Stain. A prepared ceramic colorant. A diluted coloring oxide or a blend of coloring oxide made to produce one definite color.

Stilts (or spurs, pins, etc.). Refractory clay pieces used to support ware during a glaze firing. Stilts hold ware above the kiln shelves to prevent melting glaze from sticking the ware to the shelf.

Stoneware. Pottery generally fired to a temperature between 2150° F. and 2350° F., at which the body vitrifies. A body with 0 to 5 per cent absorption and no translucency.

Translucent. Able to admit light but not transparent.

Transparent. A clear glaze resembling window glass.

Viscosity. Property of resisting flow. Stickiness. A viscous glaze flows slowly.

Vitreous. Glass-like. When a clay body is fired high enough to become non-porous, non-absorbent, hard and glossy, it has vitrified.

Volatilization. The action produced by extreme heat in a kiln in which glaze ingredients turn from a solid to a liquid and then to a gaseous state. The ingredients volatilize.

Water smoking. The beginning or first stage of firing a bisque kiln. Depending on the thickness of clay walls, the size of the pot, and how dry the pots are, the kiln should be kept below the boiling point of water for an hour, several hours or overnight. This eliminates the physically combined water. Next the temperature should increase slowly through 500° F. or 600° F. when the chemically combined water is driven off. From 900° F. to 1100° F. the temperature should rise slowly, for this is when the silica in clay changes from alpha to beta quartz, and the pot expands and may crack if it is heated too rapidly.

Wedging. A method of cutting, beating and kneading a mass of clay like bread dough to expel the air and make the whole mass homogenous. Wedging is *extremely* important. All clay should be wedged before beginning any construction process.

BIBLIOGRAPHY

REFERENCES FOR THE BEGINNER

Nelson, Glenn C., *Ceramics,* Holt, Rinehart and Winston, New York, 1960. An excellent handbook. The text is of a general nature and is written for beginning students.

Kenny, John B., *The Complete Book of Pottery Making,* Chilton Co., Philadelphia, 1949 and Greenberg Publishers, Inc., New York, 1949. A good book for beginners, well written with many illustrations of *forming* techniques.

Kenny, John B., *Ceramic Design,* Chilton Co., Philadelphia, 1963. An excellent coverage of the many ways of working with clay. Many illustrations of processes and finished articles.

Leach, Bernard, *A Potter's Book,* Faber and Faber, London, 1946, Transatlantic Arts, Hollywood-by-the-Sea, Fla., 1951. An excellent inspirational book for a more advanced student. A combination of English and Japanese techniques and ideas.

Norton, F. H., *Ceramics for the Artist-Potter,* Addison-Wesley Publishing Co., Inc., Readington, Mass., 1956. A recommended text surveying a wide range of ceramic arts from forming processes to the chemistry of glazes.

SUPPLEMENTARY REFERENCES

Eley, Vincent, *A Monk at the Potter's Wheel,* Ward, Lock & Co., Leicester, England, 1952. An account of a monk who started a pottery at his monastery, with practical information.

Wildenhain, Marguerite, *Pottery, Form and Expression,* Reinhold Publishing Corp., New York, 1959. A very inspirational book by one of America's leading women potters.

REFERENCES FOR THE ADVANCED POTTER

Hetherington, A. L., *Chinese Ceramics Glazes,* Commonwealth Press, Los Angeles, 1948. An excellent book on the chemistry of glazes, especially on the use of copper and iron as coloring materials.

Koenig, J. H., and Earhart, W. H., *Literature Abstracts of Ceramic Glazes,* College Institute, Ellenton, Fla. An excellent reference book giving condensations of all important articles on glazes in ceramic publications.

Parmelee, Cullen W., *Ceramics Glazes,* Industrial Publications, Chicago, 1951. A scholarly and comprehensive coverage of glaze materials, glazes, slips and glaze calculations.

Rhodes, Daniel, *Clay and Glazes for the Potter,* Chilton Co., Philadelphia, 1957 and Greenberg Publishers, Inc., New York, 1957. A very thorough coverage of clays, glazes and chemistry of glazes for the advanced potter.

Rhodes, Daniel, *Stoneware and Porcelain,* Chilton Co., Philadelphia, 1959. Excellent, practical studio information. A discussion of stoneware and porcelain and information on kilns.

MAGAZINES

Ceramics Monthly (4175 N. High Street,) Columbus 14, Ohio. Articles for the beginner and advanced student, hobby potter and teacher. Generally "how-to-do-it" articles, exhibitions and current events. Excellent.

Craft Horizons 29 W. 53 Street, New York 19, N.Y. This magazine covers all fields of contemporary crafts, American and foreign. Well illustrated, does not contain "how-to-do-it." Excellent.

INDEX